Quarto is the authority on a wide range of topics.

Quarto educates, entertains and enriches the lives of
our readers—enthusiasts and lovers of hands-on living.

www.quartoknows.com

First published in 2015 by Voyageur Press, an imprint of Quarto Publishing Group USA Inc.,
400 First Avenue North, Suite 400, Minneapolis, MN 55401 USA.
Telephone: (612) 344-8100 Fax: (612) 344-8692

© 2015 Quarto Publishing Group USA Inc.

quartoknows.com
Visit our blogs at quartoknows.com

Voyageur Press titles are also available at discounts in bulk quantity for industrial or sales-promotional use.
For details write to Special Sales Manager at Quarto Publishing Group USA Inc., 400 First Avenue North, Suite 400,
Minneapolis, MN 55401 USA. To find out more about our books, visit us online at www.voyageurpress.com.

Library of Congress Cataloging-in-Publication Data

Champlin, Tim, 1937-
The wild west of Louis L'Amour : an illustrated companion to the frontier fiction of an American icon / Tim Champlin.
pages cm
ISBN 978-0-7603-4688-4 (hardback)
1. L'Amour, Louis, 1908-1988--Criticism and interpretation. 2. Western stories--History and criticism.
3. West (U.S.)--In literature. 4. Heroes in literature. I. Title.
PS3523.A446Z56 2015
813'.52--dc23
2015004639

Acquisitions Editors: Steve Casper and Dennis Pernu
Art Director: Cindy Samargia Laun
Project Manager: Caitlin Fultz
Design and Layout: Ryan Scheife

Printed in China

10 9 8 7 6 5 4 3 2

Frontis: One of the most iconic Native American photographs ever taken is this image by Edward S. Curtis in 1908 in the Badlands of South Dakota. Virtually every L'Amour novel features some sort of clash with the aboriginal peoples of the continent, but rarely does he delve into their side of the story. **Contents:** To most readers in the eastern part of the United States in the 1930s, a detailed description of a southwestern desert sunset would have seemed as exotic as a trip to Egypt or China. The pulp magazines, where L'Amour's stories were first published, could take urban readers on an imaginary journey to these places for about two bits.

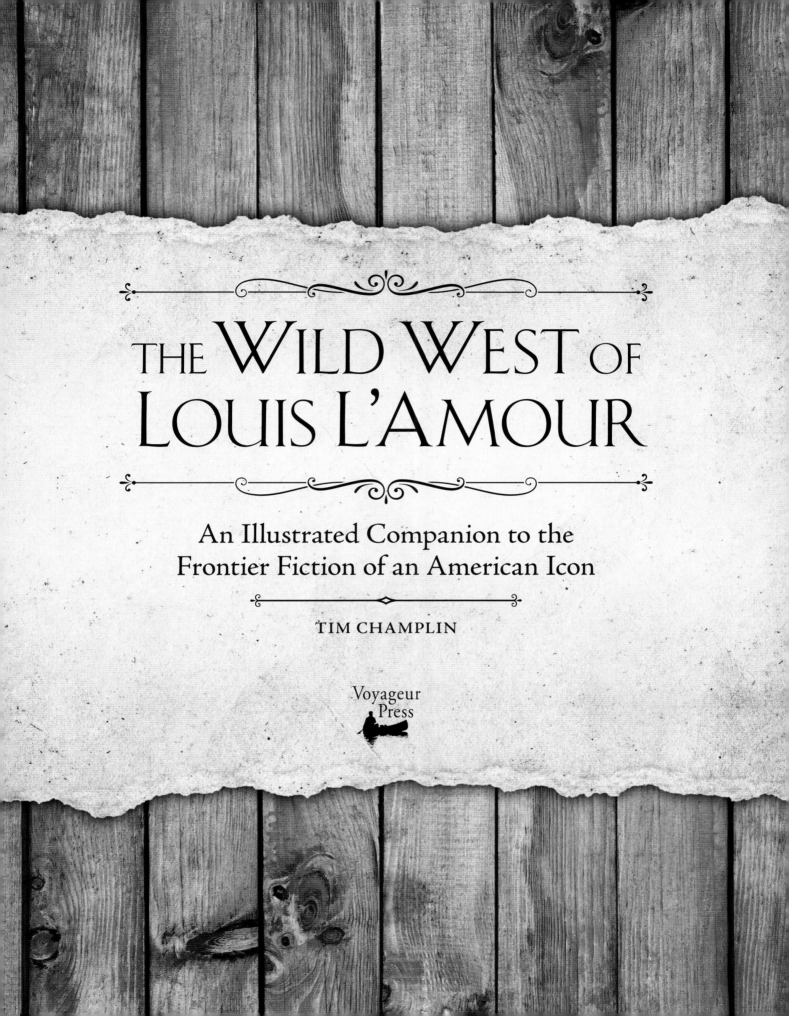

THE WILD WEST OF LOUIS L'AMOUR

An Illustrated Companion to the
Frontier Fiction of an American Icon

TIM CHAMPLIN

Voyageur
Press

To Abigail—Be proud of your achievements. We are!

CONTENTS

Foreword 7

Chapter 1
The Lay of the Land 15

Chapter 2
The Lone Rider 33

Chapter 3
Gunfighters 39

Chapter 4
Mining and Ranching 65

Chapter 5
Women 81

Chapter 6
Indians 89

Chapter 7
Reading Sign 99

Chapter 8
Food and Transportation 111

Chapter 9
Writing Style and Lingo 127

Chapter 10
Gold and Glory 141

Index 174
Photo Credits 175
About the Author 176

FOREWORD

I first saw Louis L'Amour in 1979. He had arrived in town for an interview on local television, promoting his newly published hardback novel, *Bendigo Shafte*. Determined not to miss a chance to see and hear this legend, I requested an hour of leave from my job and drove to the TV station, joining a small group of spectators in the studio to watch the talk show live.

My own western background, along with sales of a dozen articles and short stories, had given me the confidence to take a step up and try my hand at a novel set in the historic frontier. After two years of intermittent work, the novel was finished. In those precomputer days and without an agent, marketing a first novel was a slow and difficult process, especially for an unknown like myself. It involved photocopying every page of a manuscript typed on a typewriter, then mailing out a sample chapter, cover letter, and return postage to one publisher at a time. After weeks of waiting, a manila envelope would invariably show up in my mailbox containing my returned material and a printed rejection.

I'd already collected several negative responses for this novel by the time I went to see L'Amour that day. Here was a man who was not only published but was world famous. Often, the reality of seeing a living legend does not measure up to the expectation. This time it did. He was no thin, pale, bespectacled scribbler living in an isolated literary world. What I found was a six-foot-one, at least 200-pound, seventy-year-old, looking more like fifty-five, sporting a bolo tie and cowboy boots—a man who appeared every bit as rugged as the heroes in his books, a man with a background of hard work and adventure. Yet, he was soft spoken, cultured, and articulate. Being so caught up in absorbing the atmosphere of the moment, I can't recall the details of what he said about his novel. But during the interview, he emphasized the connection of his fiction with the reality of the early West.

I went back to work that day with renewed hope and energy for my own writing efforts.

The following year, on June 21, 1980, I met L'Amour in person. This time he was on a publisher-sponsored book tour of several cities. When I arrived at the shopping center for the signing, the first thing I noticed was a big bus with a huge painting of a stagecoach and six-horse hitch emblazoned on its side. L'Amour was certainly wealthy enough by this time to afford such an elaborate conveyance, but I later learned Bantam Books had furnished it for his Overland Express promotional tour.

Opposite: L'Amour used threads of his own life's experiences and wove them into details gathered from research to create novels of the West—"frontier stories" he liked to call them—that resonated with the public. Much of his research also involved reading the journals and letters of pioneers, cowboys, and lawmen.

The wagon wheels of pioneers churning their way westward set the stage for several L'Amour novels. Readers could enjoy learning the specifics of the various styles of wagons and coaches used in the Old West.

The presence of this star author brought out a big crowd. Long tables were set up to hold row after row of his paperbacks, spines upward. I finally selected two volumes of short stories to buy, then got in line. When my turn came, I introduced myself and L'Amour shook my hand. His grip engulfed mine. I told him that three months earlier Ballantine Books, a division of Random House, had accepted my first western novel for publication. He congratulated me and asked if I knew an editor friend of his, Marc Jaffe. (I didn't then, but met him two years later at a Western Writers of America convention.) Because a long line was waiting behind me, we spoke for only a few minutes. It turned out our backgrounds were eerily similar. We were born only eighty miles apart in North Dakota. We were both of French-Irish descent, and our fathers were both large animal veterinarians. I was the same age—forty-four—as he had been when an American publisher accepted his first western novel. In spite of the obvious canyon between us in age and experience, he treated me as graciously as if I were a true professional instead of a beginner. In fact, he took his felt-tipped pen and signed my book, "To Tim—All the best to a fellow writer. Louis L'Amour." At that point, he made a new fan for life.

Louis Dearborn L'Amour (1908–1988) was the most famous and best-selling author in the history of western fiction, and one of the top selling authors of all time. In the following pages we'll look at how his stories related to the real

The expansion of railroads and trains figure prominently in many tales of the Old West. This magnificent steam-powered relic resides outside of Tucson, Arizona, a virtual mecca for those interested in that period of American history.

nineteenth-century West, and then we'll examine some of the reasons he rose above all other western writers to attain his vaunted status.

The seventh child born into a middle-class family in North Dakota, he dropped out of high school at age fifteen and worked tirelessly to make a living at all kinds of laboring and factory jobs in the 1920s and 1930s, including ordinary seaman, lumber mill worker, circus roustabout, and miner. As a big, raw-boned young man who looked older than his years, he even boxed professionally for a time to augment his income. All the while, his love of learning drove him to read books on every subject—history, archeology, philosophy, and biography—during every spare minute and to attempt to write and sell short stories and poems. While

struggling through the Great Depression he sold his first short story, "Anything for a Pal," to *True Gang Life* magazine in 1935.

Drafted into the army in World War II, he served in Europe as a lieutenant with the 3622nd Quartermaster Truck Company, then settled in California, his wandering days behind him, and attempted to write for a living. By this time, his storytelling talent had been honed to a skill on the grindstone of the pulps, a few of his early adventure tales having appeared under the pen name Jim Mayo (a character he created for some of his stories).

Adventure, western, and crime fiction pulp magazines wanted stories of action that punched straight from the shoulder without bothering with such niceties as introspection, description,

Probably more than any other character of the Old West, cowboys stand tallest in most people's imaginations. Drawing from his many hours of meticulous research, Louis L'Amour was able to give his readers an idea of what a real cattle drive was like from beginning to end.

or character development. These things came later with much practice and helped round out his action plots. He used threads of his own life's experiences and wove them into details gathered from research to create novels of the West—"frontier stories," he liked to call them—that resonated with the public. The dedication in his novel *North to the Rails* acknowledged the source of much of his research: "To all the pioneers whose journals and letters have done so much to provide me with material."

Approximately thirty of his novels and stories were made into movies during his career. His protagonists exhibited a code of honor and loyalty, a never-say-die attitude, and wilderness skills combined with mental and physical toughness that brought them through the most harrowing adventures to overcome great odds. Adhering to this type of storytelling, L'Amour eventually rose to become a household name with readers around the world. At one time his publisher, Bantam Books, proudly proclaimed that a hundred million copies of his books were in print. Later in life, L'Amour received numerous prestigious awards, including a Presidential Gold Medal awarded by one of his fans, President Ronald Reagan.

People still continue to read and collect his books decades after his death.

This book will focus on L'Amour's novels and short stories, which were set in the post–Civil War American West, to discover what authentic details he borrowed and blended into his fiction—geography, well-known characters, Indian tribes, food, transportation, guns and gunfighters, lawmen, mining and prospecting, cattle rustling, the US Cavalry, and anything else connected to the actual nineteenth-century West.

"A writer is bound by no earthly ties," he wrote in his autobiography. "What he is and what he sees he creates in his mind, or his subconscious creates it for him. Thanks to the lands I have seen and the books I have read, I know what it was like.

Above top: Easily the most important wild animal of the Old West was the buffalo, or American Bison. Many Native American tribes depended solely on buffalo for survival, so when the once immense herds disappeared, the period became a sad and devastating chapter in their history. **Above bottom:** Life was harsh for people settling the Old West, and that was certainly part of the appeal for stories about them. L'Amour's own early life experiences were those of a wanderer and survivor, so one could argue that he could relate with many of his characters. **Opposite:** The spectacular landscapes of the American West were described in great detail in many of L'Amour's works. This scene from the South Dakota Badlands features a small herd of mule deer at the ridgeline.

The world of which I write is my world always. It is a claim I have staked and continue to stake, and each writer has his own way of telling a story."

CHAPTER 1

THE LAY OF THE LAND

As every western writer knows, most plots could be just as easily set east of the Mississippi in nearly any period. It's the setting—the locale, the terrain, and the lay of the land—that gives western novels their unique flavor.

Some authors of western fiction writing mainly from the 1920s through the 1940s invented landscapes for their stories. While easier than using actual places, this approach could be confusing to any readers who had even a general knowledge of the topography of the western United States—those who knew the names of rivers and mountain ranges and deserts. One author who employed this technique, a contemporary of L'Amour, was James Warner Bellah, whose unique writing style many found appealing. Bellah, though widely read, was not nearly as prolific as L'Amour. He created frontier cavalry stories that were published in the *Saturday Evening Post* in the mid-to-late 1940s.

Opposite: Some authors of western fiction invented landscapes for their stories, which was quite the opposite from the style of Louis L'Amour, who described a well-ordered world that was an accurate representation of the place and time depicted. Pictured here is Devils Tower in Wyoming with fallen basalt columns in the foreground.

Some of his short stories were even made into movies starring John Wayne (notably *Rio Grande* and *Fort Apache*), and he cowrote the screenplay for *The Man Who Shot Liberty Valance*.

Zane Grey, who was justly famous for his descriptions of the western landscape, often took a page or two to create the scene for readers. But he wrote in the early twentieth century when many readers had never seen western lands, except perhaps in *National Geographic* magazine's black-and-white photos. Or maybe they'd attended an occasional silent western movie (which might actually have been shot on the back lot of a movie studio). Grey had to devote more time to describing the setting, thus slowing the progress of his story. And Grey had a different style than L'Amour, often using five words when three would suffice.

Readers of westerns, like readers of other adventure stories, wanted escape. They wanted to be taken to a time and place long ago and far away, to be transported out of the rut of daily life. And the unfamiliar was more interesting. It represented excitement, adventure, and romance. Naturally, for some readers, the historical integrity of the setting was of secondary importance, if any importance at all. But readers who picked up a Louis L'Amour western could be assured that for a few hours they would enter a well-ordered world that was an accurate representation of the place and time depicted.

Sometimes, however, it wouldn't start out that way. L'Amour often threw his hero directly into messy circumstances, and we didn't necessarily have all the details of the time and place. Then, as the story progressed and we got a better feel for the setting, the hero might be knocked off his horse, beaten, shot, thrown over a cliff, left to bleed to death or die of thirst or cold, or at the very least, face betrayal by a woman he cared for or a relative he trusted. This protagonist's strength of body and character was what readers wanted to identify with. Now and then the hero was aided by just a little luck, but he triumphed by story's end. Readers closed the book satisfied that if this man could rise above all odds without compromising his values, then they could, too. L'Amour offered no depressing endings or antiheroes.

Often in L'Amour's westerns, the landscape also functioned not just as part of the setting but as a major character. It determined what the protagonists and antagonists could and couldn't do, and how the plot progressed. In a number of his novels, a map placed at the front of the book showed the region where the story took place. If readers were personally familiar with the area, they could visualize the surroundings even better. And if they had never been to the Painted Desert, the Grand

Below: In several books, L'Amour described some of the geologic processes that formed the spectacular terrain he was describing. Pictured is The Wave sandstone formation in the Arizona desert near the Utah border. **Opposite:** Often in L'Amour's westerns, the landscape functioned not just as part of the setting but as a major character as it determined what the protagonists and antagonists could and couldn't do and how the plot progressed. Readers would get a detailed description of scenes such as these striated, colorful rocks in Nevada's Valley of Fire region near Las Vegas.

The novel *Lando* shifted from the Appalachian Mountains to the Gulf Coast near Padre Island, Texas, with its low, sandy marsh of sea grass, salt air, tidal flats, barrier islands, and pounding surf. In each of these very different geographical settings, L'Amour brought readers smoothly along in the story, blending in descriptions of the landscape.

Canyon, or the mountains of western Montana, or even seen photos or film of such places, that was okay, too, because L'Amour described them well enough for readers to form a mental picture of what the terrain was like.

At the beginning of the novel *Lando,* Orlando Sackett began telling his story in the first person from his home in the Appalachian Mountains of east Tennessee, and L'Amour accurately described the log cabins, the small, hand-grinding grain mill, the sharpening stone, the chopping of wood for fuel, and other details of daily life there. The story later shifted to the Gulf Coast near Padre Island, Texas, with its low, sandy marsh of sea grass, salt

In the novel *Matagorda,* set on the Texas Gulf Coast, the plot was gradually overshadowed and changed by the approach of a terrible hurricane. L'Amour was very likely familiar with the famous hurricane that destroyed the town of Galveston, Texas, in 1900, and could have used details of that storm in describing his fictitious hurricane in the same area. According to the caption found on this vintage stereoscope card, the dog was trapped for forty-three days under the wreckage of the Galveston hurricane before being rescued.

The Great Plains opened up to thousands of square miles of grasslands that furnished food for vast herds of buffalo, antelope, and other herbivores. These sparse landscapes were the setting of many L'Amour novels.

air, tidal flats, barrier islands, and pounding surf. In each of these very different geographical settings, within one novel, L'Amour brought readers smoothly along in the story, blending in descriptions of the landscape.

But in another novel, *Matagorda,* also set on the Texas Gulf Coast, the lowland terrain and weather slowly took center stage. The story involved the gathering of a wild cattle herd amid a human feud, but the plot was gradually overshadowed and changed by the approach of a terrible hurricane. The hurricane destroyed the small town of Indianola and caused the plot to play out very differently than it might have otherwise. L'Amour was very likely familiar with the famous hurricane that destroyed the town of Galveston, Texas, in 1900, and could have used details of that storm in describing his fictitious hurricane in the same area.

On early maps depicting lands before American exploration and settlement had rolled beyond Missouri, cartographers, ignorant of what lay beyond the eastern edge of the Great Plains, labeled the western half of North America "The Great American Desert," a term L'Amour used in his novel, *Under the Sweetwater Rim.*

Native grasses of the eastern prairie, before they were plowed up and replaced by crops, grew three feet tall. But as one progressed beyond Illinois, Iowa, and the hardwood forests of the Mississippi Valley, the Great Plains opened up to thousands of square miles of grasslands that furnished food for vast herds of buffalo, antelope, and other herbivores. The gradual western upslope of

Top left: In the days of the great western migrations, wood for fuel and building materials was scarce. Pioneers would consider themselves lucky to travel and camp near any terrain with trees. **Top right:** Pictured is the Morrison family in front of their sod house in Custer County, Nebraska, in 1886. Lumber was scarce and sod dwellings were the first home for many pioneers. **Above:** The westward expansion of pioneers, prospectors, and in some cases criminals, during the latter half of the nineteenth century is one of the most amazing aspects of American history. This 1885 photograph captures the excitement of the time, as well as perhaps a feeling of uncertainty as to what lies ahead.

The fireplace and utensils of an old pioneer log home. Dried manure was typically used as a cooking and heating fuel on the prairie.

the plains toward the Rockies and the lessening rainfall caused the grass to be shorter and somewhat sparser as one traveled west. L'Amour used these landscapes of Kansas and Nebraska and eastern Wyoming to set several of his novels.

The Man from Skibbereen, for example, opens up with a recent Irish immigrant, Chris Mayo, accidentally missing his train and being left behind at a tiny railroad depot in the midst of vast grassland. The depot is abandoned, there is blood on the floor, and the telegraph key is chattering some unintelligible message. Thus begins a wild adventure this young foreigner must deal with while isolated in a landscape like nothing he ever saw in Ireland.

In L'Amour's novel *The Quick and the Dead,* a young couple with an eleven-year-old son were migrating west in a wagon with mules and horses. As they left the forested area of the country and emerged from under the shelter of trees, L'Amour described the feeling of vulnerability that many settlers recorded in their journals. Previously, such settlers had spent their lives in the eastern half of the United States or in Europe, where abundant trees were taken for granted. As settlers traveled along at fifteen to thirty miles a day,

the comforting presence of trees and other foliage dwindled and disappeared. It was a psychological shock. These travelers felt exposed to the elements; the wide sky arched above, and black thunderstorms could be seen eighty miles away. There was nothing to block the tornadic winds or the pelting sting of hail. Should they be stuck here, or choose to homestead on the plains, in summers they would have to deal with withering heat, plagues of grasshoppers, hailstorms, and occasional drought. In winter they'd endure bitter temperatures, frozen creeks, blizzards with drifting snow borne on endless prairie wind, and the ache of loneliness that came from living in such an isolated place. (O. E. Rolvaag's novel *Giants in the Earth* is an excellent depiction of the hardships Dakota pioneers endured.)

Today, it is easy to spot farm and ranch houses from a distance on the plains because windbreaks of protective trees have long since been planted around them. In the days of the great western migrations, however, wood for fuel and building materials was not often at hand on the vast open country. To even kindle a campfire, travelers were forced to scrounge what dry sticks or driftwood they could find along streams such as the Platte River. Frequently, people on preceding wagon trains had stripped the countryside for miles on either side of major trails where these first highways crossed the Great Plains. Later migrants had to burn dried manure and often slung pieces of canvas beneath their wagons to carry along the flattened dung of oxen or horses. The absence of wood forced early settlers in Nebraska and Kansas to live in south-facing dugouts cut into hillsides or in houses built from chunks of prairie sod bound together with the tough roots of the native grasses.

In *Hanging Woman Creek,* set in the northern plains of 1885 Montana, L'Amour described one of his itinerant heroes, along with a black former boxer, riding a freight car toward Miles City,

The lowly tumbleweed actually played a role in the novel *Conagher*. Tumbleweeds originate from several different kinds of small shrubs that, when mature, dry out, break off from their roots, and roll away on the wind.

looking for temporary work as cowhands. (This was an experience taken directly from his youth, when he'd ridden a freight car with a black boxer.) L'Amour was aware that the rails, by the time of this story, had been laid across the northern plains. He described the gently undulating terrain of eastern Montana accurately, and even mentioned late summer wheat fields ripening into golden grain. In this story, he also used real towns and real pioneers (such as cattleman Granville Stuart).

In the story, the two friends knew they were running into trouble of some sort involving rustlers and land grabbers. But they needed work and took a winter job caring for a herd of beef cattle grazing on the thick grama and buffalo grass of the open range. The pair holed up in a well-stocked line shack to ride out the cold months. They were experienced at this, and when the blizzards came, they not only dealt with the weather, but with rustlers, too. They knew their environment and could tell

how deep an earlier snow had been by the height of the grizzly claw marks on the trees. They knew the tracks of wolves, elk, and deer. When a large portion of their herd went missing, they knew the animals hadn't just wandered off on the open grassland because cattle did not graze in a straight line. They had been rustled, and the partners went after the cattle, following their massive trail, and the hoof prints of the rustlers' shod horses.

The novel *Conagher* was set where the western plains began to transition into higher, drier country, and L'Amour used an unusual feature of the land—tumbleweeds—to draw the hero, Conn Conagher, to a lonely widow, Evie Teale. Tumbleweeds originate from several different kinds of small shrubs that, when mature, dry out, break off from their roots, and roll away on the wind.

Evie, who had two children, was trying to make a go of an isolated homestead after her husband was lost. Evie was lonely and had taken to

Left: Some of the young nation's best, untouched locations were along the eastern base of the Rockies, where grass, water, and wood were abundant. In the foothills, short grass gave way to subalpine meadows, wildflowers, and groves of aspen. **Below:** As his stories unfolded, L'Amour's verbal paintbrush filled the readers' minds with such details as yellow-bellied marmots, blue grouse, and other western creatures like the roadrunner—animals that would have been foreign to city dwellers on the east coast who may never have had the chance to travel far.

writing short, unsigned notes about her feelings and attaching them to tumbleweeds, much like someone putting a message in a bottle and tossing it into the ocean. The tumbleweeds blew across the level land for miles, only to fetch up against a fence or barn. Conagher found several of these little white pieces of paper tied to the dry weeds and read the brief notes. One of them said, "Sometimes when I am alone I feel I will die if I don't talk to someone, and I am alone so much. I love to hear the wind in the grass or in the cedars." Conagher saved the notes and, while working as a ranch hand, inquired among the scattered inhabitants of the region until he finally discovered who the woman was. They eventually became acquainted when he rescued her and the children

In many novels, L'Amour's characters kept themselves oriented by sighting on familiar landmarks. Pictured is Helmcken Falls after an early winter storm, in Wells Gray Park, British Columbia, Canada.

L'Amour apparently loved silent, lonely places—the vast, arid distances of sand and rugged, treeless mountains covering the southern half of present-day New Mexico, Arizona, and California, as well as a good portion of northern Mexico.

from marauding Indians. In spite of their completely different personalities, they marry.

Beyond the Great Plains, the Rocky Mountains rear their rugged bulk to block or invite pioneers. Just as with the plains, L'Amour's work shows intimate familiarity with mountain terrain. In several of his novels, including *The Quick and the Dead*, L'Amour wrote of settlers, often young men, seeking their fortunes and looking for land to settle for ranching.

Some of the young nation's best, untouched locations at that time were along the eastern base of the Rockies, where grass, water, and wood were abundant. In the foothills, short grass gave way to subalpine meadows and wildflowers. As his stories unfolded, L'Amour's verbal paintbrush filled the readers' minds with such details as yellow-bellied marmots, blue grouse, and deer. He identified ragwort and monkey grass, aspens, groves of golden cinquefoil, and growths of columbine.

Moving into a mountain setting for his novel *Under the Sweetwater Rim*, L'Amour described a harrowing escape of the protagonist and his friends. Being pursued by killers just above timberline, they were forced to traverse several hundred yards diagonally across a steep, exposed field of loose shale where the weight of a horse, or even a man afoot, could cause the unstable rock to slide toward a precipice.

L'Amour wrote in detail of certain passes and particular peaks, of caves in the rocks, of thunder echoing off the mountainsides, and of passes

This period color map, entitled "Map No 7, the Territorial Growth of the United States, 1783–1866," shows the country's westward expansion and illustrates the notion of Manifest Destiny. It was created in 1898 by British publisher Longmans, Green, & Co, and engraved by New York–based Struthers & Co.

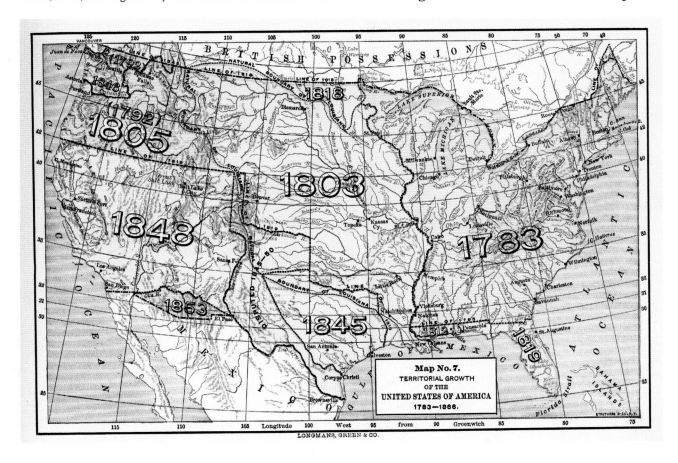

partially blocked by snow even in summer. In *Under the Sweetwater Rim*, a cavalry officer, Lieutenant Ten Brian, has rescued several people from a wagon train massacre and fled with them into the high mountains. During a pause to rest, he gave a lady companion a geological explanation of how the mountains of the story's setting were formed and were still being shaped, slowly, over eons of time.

In the huge wilderness of the Rockies, traveling men were forced to limit their routes to the trails that had been found, through trial and error, over many years by animals, Indians, and mountain men. Some of these passes through high country later became rail beds and highways. Routes in rough terrain were dictated by the lay of the land.

Mounted men, and especially those with wagons, were compelled to seek out the easiest routes, whether through a known pass, skirting a hill, or following a valley.

L'Amour's men often used peaks and mountains with familiar shapes as landmarks to keep from becoming lost. In the early pages of *Taggart*, a rider spotted the distinctive shape of Squaw Peak and rode up onto a higher elevation from where he could see the Salt River, thus pegging him east of the small town of Phoenix, Arizona, and allowing him to determine the direction to the mountain town of Globe. In this novel, L'Amour's characters kept themselves oriented by sighting on the massive bulk of Rockinstraw Mountain (in present Gila County), visible for miles.

In *Last Stand at Papago Wells*, a huge dust storm interrupts a pivotal battle. L'Amour deftly describes a roiling cloud of brown dust and sand hundreds of feet high as it boils across the desert floor. Those who don't take cover quickly will find their eyes and noses filled with dust, their teeth gritty, and a suffocating sensation gripping their chests.

Above: The availability of water in the Old West was a life or death situation and became a typical plot point in many of L'Amour's novels. Finding a natural source from afar can at times be refreshingly obvious as in the case of Palm Canyon, part of the Indian Canyons in the Agua Caliente Indian Reservation, near Palm Springs, California. **Left:** Shallow pools of rainwater cupped in worn hollows of rock were known as "tanks." L'Amour referred to one of the better-known tanks, *Tinajas Altas,* which still exists (and is pictured here) in a low desert mountain between Yuma and Papago Wells, a few miles north of the Mexican border.

As one would expect of a writer of westerns, nearly all of L'Amour's works were based on various groups of people settling the new territories. This interesting 1873 print by George Crofutt shows an allegorical female figure of America leading pioneers westward, as they travel on foot, in a stagecoach, Conestoga wagon, and by railroads, where they encounter Native Americans and herds of bison.

Moving southwestward across the continent, a nineteenth-century migrant would have eventually encountered the arid desert region where L'Amour set many of his novels and short stories. He knew the area well, and his descriptions of the stark landscape were very similar to those of his contemporary western writer, Gordon D. Shirreffs. Both men apparently loved those silent, lonely places—the vast, arid distances of sand and rugged, treeless mountains covering the southern half of present-day New Mexico, Arizona, and California, as well as a good portion of northern Mexico.

Just as in writing sea stories where the setting looks the same now as it did in Viking times, placing stories in the unoccupied southwestern deserts presents the reader with a timeless landscape that requires no stretch of the imagination.

By the latter half of the 1800s, the terrain there had been explored and mapped but not widely occupied by white settlers, who were scattered here and there, mostly on fortified ranches and a few small towns. Keepers of solitary, widely spaced stage stations led a precarious existence in the land of the hostiles, even though the government attempted to provide some protection for travelers and settlers by locating a handful of cavalry posts at strategic locations.

For the most part, however, the land was still claimed by Apaches and a few of the more settled tribes such as the Navajo, Pima, and the Pueblos. Even without these tribes who had called the region home for centuries, the land itself was a deterrent to white settlement. Waterless and treeless, with extreme temperatures, home to strange plants and animals, the sandy soil requiring irrigation to grow crops, the Mojave Desert and its low, jagged mountain ranges were considered by many a wasteland not worth fighting for. The cavalry was equally out of place here, not at all equipped to deal with the land or its natives.

Thus, in *Last Stand at Papago Wells*, a disparate group of whites find themselves isolated at the three water holes of the title and surrounded by Apaches determined to wipe them out before any outside help can arrive. A leather-tough lone rider named Logan Cates assumes command and helps the settlers defend themselves while holding onto the lifesaving water and the rocky fortified position for days. When the defenders are finally beaten down to their last reserves, weakened by infighting and the Apaches, desperate with hunger and fatigue, they are saved by a violent sandstorm that drives off their remaining attackers.

Such storms blow up without warning in the region. A roiling cloud of brown dust and sand hundreds of feet high boils across the desert floor. Unlike normal summer storms, no thunder or lightning heralds its silent, unnerving approach. A dirty cloud envelops everything in a blast of wind-driven sand that stings exposed skin. Even the paint on modern vehicles can be sandblasted down to shiny metal. Those who don't take cover quickly will find their eyes and noses filled with dust, their teeth gritty, and a suffocating sensation gripping

The immense mesas of western lands worked their way into many of L'Amour's tales. Pueblo Indians at Acoma (in present-day New Mexico near the Rio Grande River) built their towns atop such mesas for protection.

their chests. Lungs fight for clean air in the smothering atmosphere.

L'Amour knew his weather, and so did the Apache attackers in *Last Stand at Papago Wells*, who retreated from the fury of the sandstorm to fight another day when the odds were more in their favor. Papago Wells still exists just where L'Amour placed it in his novel. It was a vital source of water for both Indians and white travelers.

Besides reliable natural wells or springs, other waterholes in the southern deserts were temporary and seasonal shallow pools known as "tanks"— rainwater cupped in worn hollows of rock, usually in some of the low, rugged mountains. Tanks retained rainwater for as long as it took the heat to evaporate them. These stagnant pools, sometimes holding hundreds of gallons, were often rank with algae and breeding insects, and sometimes holding feces from small animals that came to drink. The water could save life in an emergency but could also make a human quite sick. L'Amour referred to one

of the better-known tanks—*Tinajas Altas,* literally, "High Tanks,"—which were partially shaded natural layers of rock with hollow depressions scoured out over eons by wind and sand. For days (or weeks, if they were full enough) they could retain whatever rainwater fell during brief cloudbursts. But tanks were unreliable. Any traveler was wise not to bet his life on them containing water, especially in the drier months. *Tinajas Altas,* located in a low desert mountain between Yuma and Papago Wells, and a few miles north of the Mexican border, were only accessible by foot. A man had to climb steep, slick rocks to reach them. They were a long way from anywhere, like a lifesaving island in the midst of a vast ocean of desert.

Besides just the undulating, eroded deserts, mesas figured prominently in L'Amour's frontier fiction. A *mesa* (Spanish for table) was a flat-topped butte, usually thrusting up vertically from the desert floor around it. A mesa could be of any size, but many had walls several hundred feet high

Much of the Southwest was waterless and treeless, a hostile environment to most travelers, but the spectacular geography of the area was like nothing seen in the eastern half of the country.

and their nearly level tops covered hundreds of acres. The largest mesas were several miles in circumference. Frequently published photos of the "mittens" in Monument Valley, Arizona, (where several John Ford westerns were filmed) show two large, well-formed mesas.

Pueblo Indians at Acoma (in present-day New Mexico near the Rio Grande River) built their towns atop such mesas for protection. They climbed up and down steep trails to tend their irrigated crops on the valley floor, and, for many generations, remained safe. But in the 1600s they were finally conquered by Spanish troops from Mexico.

As the Acoma Indians discovered, mesas were not always perfectly formed, with vertical walls that defied climbing. Over long periods of time, rock weathered and split, creating slopes where

foot trails could be hacked out. Rock falls, and the rubble of jumbled boulders at the bottom, could even allow horses to ascend. For example, in L'Amour's short story "Riding On," the mounted hero tracked a band of rustlers in rough country. Clued by a scratch on a rock and his own hunch, he rode on and, "It led him into the broken rock of the shattered canyon wall, and then onto a green topped mesa." He finally found their hiding place. "Day was just breaking in the east when he first found the opening into Dark Canyon and rode down from the lip of the mesa into the deep, shadowy green recesses of this oasis in the desert."

In *The Man Called Noon*, protagonist Ruble Noon and the girl he's trying to protect, Fan Davidge, were fleeing from a gang of killers. Noon found a long tunnel that penetrated a mesa. When

Membership in wagon trains was generally fluid; an accident or illness, for instance, might have forced someone to fall behind and wait for the next train. Some broke away to settle in the Colorado Territory or other territories along the way.

the tunnel emerged on the other side, there was only a sheer drop-off of several hundred feet. In the split rock above them, he found a narrow chimney three to four feet wide that ran all the way to the top. He and Fan climbed this by using tiny toeholds and handholds and wedging themselves into the chute. The outlaws finally caught up and began firing upward at them. Noon shot back, and he and the girl dropped rocks to discourage pursuit. They finally reached the top safely where they found the ruins of an ancient village on several level acres. The girl feared they were trapped on top, but Noon said, "There's got to be a way. I've seen some steep-walled mesas, but never one that couldn't be scaled, either up or down."

They finally found a big *V*-shaped notch in the mesa top on the far side filled with boulders and trees and the next day used this steep, crumbling gash to make their escape to the bottom.

L'Amour set a few of his novels in the eastern and southern United States, but western settings are featured in the bulk of his work. His stories play out from the home of the Sackett clan in the east Tennessee Appalachian Mountains all the way across to the West Coast.

Even though the action in *Mojave Crossing* begins with a chase across the desert, it eventually comes to a ranch in southern California and the latter part of the book takes place in and around what would later become the megalopolis of Los Angeles, giving the reader a good idea of what that area looked like before all the small towns grew together in the development sprawl of the twentieth century.

The deep wilderness of the Old West provided the
perfect environment for the quintessential lone rider.
Though L'Amour did not start the tradition of the lone
rider, he certainly continued it with considerable gusto.

CHAPTER 2

THE LONE RIDER

Nearly all of L'Amour's novels were morality plays where good triumphed over evil. Rarely were there any shades of gray.

'Amour did not start the tradition of the lone rider, but he certainly continued it with considerable gusto. This lone-riding, courageous, quiet man talked with his fists and his guns, came from who-knew-where, and when he rode into view, curiosity quickly gave way to hate or apprehension on the part of the bad guys, and hope and relief for those oppressed. This hero, who became a cliché in novels and movies over the years following Owen Wister's novel *The Virginian* in 1902, was the person a reader or viewer automatically identified with. This lone rider was the precursor to the superhero of today, except the lone rider, though skilled and courageous, stayed within human capabilities; he had no superhuman powers. He was the same unfettered, self-reliant, capable man who was depicted by Clint Eastwood in Sergio Leone's "Spaghetti Westerns." This was the lone rider, probably twenty-five to forty years of age, hard, lean, and hungry, carrying the burden of an unknown past that was as mysterious as his sudden appearance. From the look of him, he bore scars of past battles, and maybe even a lost love. His squinting blue-green eyes had seen much and looked upon the world with tolerant wisdom. He was dignified and calm—until forced to act. Then he struck like a deadly rattler. Whatever situation he rode into, be it a crooked sheriff, a wealthy land-grabber, outlaw claim-jumpers, night riders harassing sodbusters, a protection racket enforced by a gang of bullies, the reader or viewer knew from the outset the bad guys would get their comeuppance. Sometimes the reader was introduced to him as he was fleeing a posse or a gang of outlaws, and he had to call on all his wilderness skills and endurance to elude them.

It was a morality play where good triumphed over evil. There were no shades of gray.

His novel *Kilkenny* began in such a way: "To Clifton House on the Canadian came a lone rider on a long-legged buckskin. He was a green-eyed man wearing a flat-crowned, flat-brimmed black hat, black shirt and chaps. The Barlow & Sanderson Stage had just pulled in when the rider came out of the lava country, skirting the hills of the *Sangre de Cristos*.

"He was riding easy when they first saw him but his horse was dust-coated and the sweat had dried on him. The man had a tear in his shirt-sleeve and a bloody bandage on his side. He rode directly to the stable and dismounted, caring first for his horse."

Wouldn't a sight like that grab your attention?

On the first page of *Last Stand at Papago Wells,* the reader was introduced to Logan Cates, the type of hero L'Amour liked to write about:

"Logan Cates had the look of the desert about him, a brown, seasoned man with straight black hair above a triangular face that was all bone and tight-drawn, sun-browned hide. His eyes, narrow from squinting into sun and wind, were a cold green that made a man stop and think before he looked into them a second time.

"He was a tall man, wide in the shoulder and lean in waist and hips, an easy-moving man with none of the horseman's awkwardness in walking. He moved like a hunter when on his own feet, and had been a hunter of many things, men not the least among them."

The reader knew right away that this man had the makings.

And again, on page one of *Kilrone,* the reader met a man with a different name, but of the same type:

"The rider was unshaven, and the dark hair curled around his ears and over the collar of his

Clint Eastwood in Sergio Leone's "Spaghetti Western" films typified the same unfettered, self-reliant, capable man who was depicted in many L'Amour westerns. He was dignified and calm—until forced to act. Then he struck like a deadly rattler.

sun-bleached shirt. When he swung down she noted the gun hung low, the narrow hips, and the powerful shoulders. His hat brim was ragged, and there was a bullet hole through the crown.

"When he was a few paces from her she could clearly see the line of an old scar on his cheekbone. His lean brown face was haggard, and in his eyes was the daze of a dreadful weariness. On the collar and shoulder of his faded blue shirt was a dark stain of dried blood."

The reader would be hooked. Who was this guy and what has been happening to him?

Especially in his earlier, shorter books, L'Amour continued his tradition of the short stories he

The main characters in a L'Amour story were the precursors to the superheroes of today, except these riders, though skilled and courageous, stayed within human capabilities; they had no superhuman powers.

wrote for the pulps. But then he began to expand on his themes somewhat, and his plots became a bit more involved. The main characters were fleshed out. They grew introspective, thinking about their past, where they were headed, and their hopes and dreams for the future in a new land. Although good still triumphed in the end, L'Amour introduced more three-dimensional, complex characters—characters who had weaknesses as well as strengths.

Now and then one of his minor characters who was going down the wrong trail in the beginning, or who was following a crowd of dubious integrity, slowly began to see the light, and by the end of the story, had changed, rejected his wrong-headed friends, and showed decency and the courage to do right. Such a man appeared in *The Man from Skibbereen*. "The fellow looked down at him ... He held out his hand. 'You'll shake? I'm sorry I shot at you. That's the trouble with this country, a man

never knows who he's shooting. I'm Parry Blessing. I rode out of Dundaff in Pennsylvania too long ago ... I fought it [the Civil War] out, and here I am, a man scarce thirty with a feeling that death is on him. All from bad companions, like they say!'"

Drawing from his own past as a boxer, L'Amour several times created a protagonist who was good with his fists. An example of this was in *The Iron Marshal*, where protagonist Tom Shanaghy was a former New York street brawler.

In *Hanging Woman Creek,* a professional black middleweight taught the protagonist, Barnabas Pike, the tricks of fist fighting. Pike learned his lessons well, and put them to good use against an outlaw later in the story.

Even one who was not a trained boxer, such as Ten Brian in *Under the Sweetwater Rim,* could handle himself in a desperate rough-and-tumble fight to the death with Reuben Kelsey, a bigger, stronger opponent. In the midst of this boxing,

Above left: The Louis L'Amour lone rider, probably twenty-five to forty years of age, hard, lean, and hungry, carried the burden of an unknown past that was as mysterious as his sudden appearance. **Above right:** One could easily argue that many a Hollywood director and actor may have been influenced by a L'Amour novel or two by analyzing their depictions of wild west protagonists. **Opposite:** The detritus of the Civil War loomed large in the Old West for several decades. Pictured is Quantrill Raider George Maddox who was a guerilla on the side of the Rebels during the war, escaped from prosecution in Missouri, and moved to Nevada.

wrestling, gouging fight, L'Amour wrote, "Brian broke loose, feinted, and when Kelsey came in, met his rush with a right to the wind." He used this expression twice in the same scene, meaning a right to the midsection—a body punch designed to knock the breath out of an opponent. L'Amour apparently never took part in organized sports, except for boxing, but he used his experience to great effect in many of his books.

The hero, Barnes Kilrone, took on the formidable Iron Dave Sproul in a no-holds-barred fight at the end of the novel *Kilrone*. In an epic battle that L'Amour took six pages to describe, Kilrone barely beat the villain, finally knocking him unconscious. Sproul, knowing his fearsome reputation was done and no one would be cowed by him again, took his gold and two horses and rode out before the law could arrest him for gun-running to the Indians. In an ironic twist at the end, Medicine Dog, the brutal Bannock war chief who had bought guns from Sproul, ambushed and killed the big man to steal his horses.

CHAPTER 3

GUNFIGHTERS

The frontier, by its very nature, always moved ahead of set laws and established order. Those who forged ahead of human settlement to explore mountains and wide open spaces had to create their own law until civilization caught up with them, usually several years after the pioneers had clashed with Indians, harsh environments, and each other. This was true from the time European settlers arrived on the east coast of North America and began to push inland in numbers after the American Revolution.

In L'Amour's novel *North to the Rails,* a man who ran a stage station was advising newcomer Tom Chantry on the wisdom of going armed. "Out here there's nothin' but local law, and a man can be as mean as he wants to until folks catch up with him, or until he meets some bigger, tougher man. This is raw country; the good folks are good because it's their nature, and the bad can run to meanness until somebody fetches them up short. That's why you'd better arm yourself. If you're goin' to be in this country you'll need a gun."

Between 1848 and the mid-1850s, thousands of prospectors who flocked to the gold fields of California had to create their own rules in conformity to decent human conduct and good order. They had to then enforce those rules against claim jumpers, bullies, armed robbers, and those

Left: In *North to the Rails,* a man who ran a stage station was advising a newcomer on the ways of the frontier. "Out here there's nothin' but local law, and a man can be as mean as he wants to until folks catch up with him, or until he meets some bigger, tougher man. This is raw country; the good folks are good because it's their nature, and the bad can run to meanness until somebody fetches them up short."
Opposite: Those who forged ahead of human settlement to explore mountains and wide open spaces had to create their own law until civilization caught up with them. This aspect of the Old West would of course be an attraction to men possessing less-than-honorable intentions.

Top left: Prospectors heading to the Klondike near the turn of the century found that the established Canadian law was stretched too thin to adequately police that frozen wilderness. To maintain order, the stampeders formed miners' courts, and certain basic rules were enforced. **Top right:** Gold prospectors starting the 1,400-mile journey home from Alaska in the spring of 1899. **Above:** Backpackers circa 1898 as men explore Alaska to seek their fortune. Unfortunately very few ever hit it big.

Above left: When a man carried everything he owned on his back and his burro, he was vulnerable to all sorts of thievery in the relatively lawless desert lands and mountain wilderness of the Old West. This silver ore prospector was photographed near Tucson, Arizona, in 1880. **Above right:** Vigilantes summarily hanged outlaws who were caught committing serious crimes such as armed robbery, horse theft, rustling, or murder after a short trial that usually didn't include the right of appeal. Drunkenness was not considered a legitimate defense.

who would murder for profit. California had only recently been acquired from Mexico and wouldn't become a state until 1850, and United States law enforcement officers were scarce.

The same thing happened in the Klondike fifty years later when established Canadian law was stretched too thin to adequately police that frozen wilderness. To maintain order, the stampeders formed miners' courts, and certain basic rules enforced. For those cheating gamblers, robbers, thieves, rustlers, and killers, groups of the more stable and courageous men voluntarily came together and formed Committees of Vigilance to police the camps and early towns. These vigilantes usually acted under cover of masks or darkness to throw fear into undesirable troublemakers. A written warning was often posted in a public place advising all thieves, bunko steerers, card sharks, and bullies to leave town by a certain time and date. If strong hints and threats didn't scare petty criminals into leaving, stronger action was taken. Lacking proper jails, punishments such as public whippings and tarring and feathering were used. Those outlaws who

were caught committing more serious crimes such as armed robbery, horse theft, rustling, or murder were summarily hanged after a short trial that usually didn't include the right of appeal. Drunkenness was not considered a legitimate defense.

Two of the more famous groups of vigilantes operated in 1850s San Francisco and in the gold camps of Montana about a decade later. As in any human justice system where unchecked power is given to a few, corruption crept in, and the vigilantes in time began to overreact, punishing their enemies and even using their power for political motives. Vigilante justice, with its potential for abuse, was abolished within a few short years after it had served its purpose, giving way to a legitimate court system.

At the end of the novel *The Man from Skibbereen*, after the leaders of an outlaw gang were dispatched, L'Amour mentioned that vigilantes in town got rid of the remaining members of the Parley gang.

In such an environment where thousands of strangers from all over the world were thrown

Above: Wagon trains of emigrants moving west had to rely upon the gunfighting skills of their trail leaders and members of their party in the event of an attack from Native Americans or thieves. Long rifles would certainly have a huge advantage over pistols in a scenario such as this. **Opposite:** A Mormon vigilante aims his gun at a pioneer wagon during the Mountain Meadows Massacre of 1857 in southern Utah, which claimed the lives of 120 men, women, and children making their way from Arkansas to California. Today historians attribute the tragic massacre to a combination of factors, including war hysteria about possible invasion of Mormon territory and hyperbolic Mormon teachings against outsiders, which were part of the excesses of the Mormon Reformation period.

together in boomtowns and gold camps, where wolves, rattlesnakes, mountain lions, hostile Indians, and white criminals were an ever-present danger, men wore guns for protection as a routine thing. Carrying rifles, pistols, and knives openly was not considered unusual. On the contrary, if a man in the American West of the mid to late nineteenth century was not seen to be armed, it was a lack to be remarked upon. In L'Amour's novel

North to the Rails, Tom Chantry went west to buy cattle. He was against violence, and chose to go unarmed. Two bandits, riding double and fleeing a robbery, came upon Chantry on a lonely trail. "Hand said, 'You notice somethin' peculiar? This gent ain't wearin' no gun.'

" 'Rough country,' Bud commented. 'If'n I was you, mister, I'd wear a gun. You never know who you'll meet up with.'

Upper left: In a scene in *Kilrone*, hundreds of Indians attacked an undermanned cavalry fort, and the few defenders were making a stand in an adobe building. Lower left: Actors dressed as post-Civil War African-American Cavalry soldiers stand at attention during a hands-on Civil War learning experience at Delaney Farm in Aurora, Colorado. At the time, these troops were better known as the buffalo soldiers due to the long buffalo coats many wore in the wintertime. Opposite: After the Civil War, many rebel soldiers left the devastated economy of the south and moved west for a new life, carrying whatever possessions they could. In most cases that would be a rifle or pistol left over from the war.

"Chantry shrugged. 'I don't wear a gun. If you'll pardon my saying so, I think guns lead to trouble.'"

The bandits took advantage of the situation and robbed him of his horse and gear.

Even the so-called "sodbusters" who came west individually or by wagon train following the mountain men and earlier pioneers, carried rifles and shotguns for hunting abundant game for food, and for self-protection. Firearms were considered essential tools.

Any author attempting to write novels of the American frontier had to know considerable details about the weapons that were carried and used.

Louis L'Amour knew his firearms and he knew history. In a scene in *Kilrone,* for example, hundreds of Indians attacked an undermanned cavalry fort, and the few defenders were making a stand in an adobe building. Four or five Bannocks managed to penetrate the overhead attic. Kilrone heard the Indians and knew they could open the trapdoor and drop down inside. He gave orders for his few men to aim their rifles at the ceiling three feet apart and fire a volley in unison, then take one step forward and fire again, and then repeat the process once more. He knew the rifles held within a couple feet of the ceiling had enough power to penetrate the one-inch planks and kill most of the hidden attackers.

After the bloody upheaval of the Civil War, thousands of young ex-soldiers, especially Southerners, found themselves adrift, having lost land, homes or family members. They were glad to have survived. Many of them, rather than trying to pick up the pieces of their lives and rebuild in the ruined economy of the South, chose to take what they could carry and migrate west to seek a new start. The Old South was gone. Reconstruction had begun and many of the middle and lower class former Confederates decided not to face humiliating martial law and property-grabbing carpetbaggers the law now protected. It was time to go, and they went by the thousands, carrying with them whatever property they still owned, often only a horse or mule and a sidearm or two consisting of a cap and ball pistol or musket. They had fought a war with these guns and the now-disbanded Confederate Army had no use for weapons. Thus it was that the

Left: For criminals in the Old West, having their photograph taken could be a dangerous, and ultimately fatal decision, especially when the law decided to put a price on their head. **Above:** Card games were an important part of the western scene and were in fact the occasional cause of gunplay. Many towns however, forbade the carrying of arms upon entry, limiting most saloon brawls to fisticuffs. **Opposite:** Frank (left) and Jesse James were two former rebel guerillas from Missouri's Quantrill Raiders who made their way west to head one of the most notorious gangs of the time, virtually inventing the art of organized train and bank robberies. Their exploits were recorded in print at the time they were alive, and they are still being written about today.

West, after 1865, began to fill up with armed men who knew how to use the guns they carried.

In spite of the vigilance committees that were formed here and there, the majority of men on the frontier knew they had to protect themselves, their families, and their property for the time being. It wasn't just the honest homesteaders and settlers who were streaming into the western plains, mountains, and deserts. Men fleeing west from the law east of the Mississippi found the vast territories convenient places to hide, and the scattered populations, prospectors, saloons, stores, and banks easier prey without the constant threat of an organized and watchful police force. It would be years in many cases before civilization caught up with the lawbreakers who enjoyed the relative freedom to commit crime. To their way of

thinking, it was a time and place where the strong survived and the weak perished. To judge from their actions, "Might made Right."

CIVIL WAR

So, what kinds of weapons were used by both the law-abiding and the lawless? We've mentioned the ex-Confederates who carried mostly cap and ball revolvers they had kept after the war. Actually, a bewildering number of makes, models, and calibers of rifles, revolvers, and muskets were used on both sides during the Civil War. The South didn't have the manufacturing capabilities of the northern gun makers. The Confederacy did produce a few makes such as Spiller & Burr, Leech & Rigdon, Griswold and Gunnison, and Dance and

Parks. Because of the scarcity of steel, these weapons were made with brass frames. They very much resembled the Colt or the Remington in looks, size, and function.

Some Confederate soldiers brought their own guns from home when they joined up; others were issued one long gun each of various makes and models. Lack of uniformity was not the problem then that it became later in the era of the self-contained cartridge. During the war, men carried bullet molds and could fashion their own lead projectiles when they ran out. Loose black powder was supplied, as were the small copper caps that set off the charge. A measure of powder was poured down the barrel or into the front of the revolver cylinders, a lead bullet added, then seated with a ramrod or loading lever. A cap fit on a nipple at the rear of each revolver chamber, or under the hammer of a single-shot rifle. The hammer striking the fulminate of mercury cap would set off the black powder and fire the bullet. Weapons were dropped by the hundreds during many of the bloody battles, so northern rifles, and often handguns, wound up in the hands of soldiers who were on the lookout for something better than what they already had.

The Confederate government purchased a large number of weapons from England. Thus, the British-made Beaumont-Adams came into use by many of the Southern enlisted men. Officers on both sides were expected to furnish their own sidearms and many also chose this well-made double-action pistol.

Wealthier individuals on both sides could raise and pay a volunteer company, appoint themselves as captain, and even furnish the men with horses and weapons. Those lucky enough to serve under a generous wealthy man were even sometimes equipped with the latest Henry repeating rifles, the successor of the early Volcanic rifle and the forerunner of the Winchester. This rifle, with the bright brass receiver, had an octagonal barrel and fired a .44 caliber rimfire cartridge. The Henry was loaded by twisting open a section of a loading tube under the barrel near the muzzle. The cartridges—sixteen of them—were then slid down inside the loading tube and the tube twisted shut. The lever under the stock was worked to load a round into the chamber, cocking the hammer, and the gun was ready to fire. Some Southerners who were using mostly single-shot rifled muskets or smoothbores called the Henry, "That damned Yankee rifle you can load on Sunday and shoot all week."

The Henry evolved into its successor, the 1866 model Winchester lever action. This later gun can be distinguished at a glance from the longer Henry because, even though it had the same bright yellow brass receiver, it was made with a wooden forearm to provide a steadying grip without burning the hand on a hot barrel. The model 1866 Winchester, nicknamed the "Yellow Boy," became a favorite of many of the western Indians who decorated the stocks with tacks in various designs.

continued on page 56

Opposite, top of page: In the film *Unforgiven*, Clint Eastwood utilized a Spencer carbine (pictured below; here he is brandishing a double-barrel shotgun), which was a shorter and lighter version of the Spencer rifle. **Opposite left:** A Civil War infantry .56-caliber Spencer repeating rifle M 1860, which was manufactured in Boston and featured rimfire cartridges. The Spencer was adopted by the Union Army, especially by the cavalry, during the American Civil War, but did not replace the standard issue muzzle-loading rifled muskets in use at the time. **Opposite right:** The .45-caliber Colt 1873 revolver has long been considered "The Gun that Won the West." It was also known as the Colt Single Action, Peacemaker, or Frontier and came in .44-40 and .32-20 calibers for the civilian market. Commercial production ceased in 1941 but soon came back into production in the 1950s due to the demand by the TV and film industry for Wild West–era guns. Pictured is an early cap-and-ball black-powder version of the Colt with an open top frame. **Opposite below:** Winchester had the basic design of the Henry rifle completely modified and improved to become the first Winchester rifle, the Model 1866. It fired the same .44 caliber rimfire cartridges as the Henry but had an improved magazine and, for the first time, a wooden forearm. Both rifles shared a unique double firing pin which struck the head of the rimfire cartridge in two places when the weapon was fired.

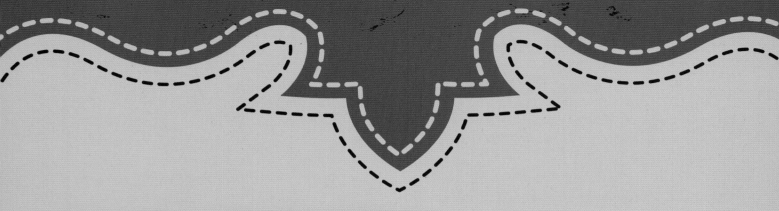

FIREARMS DEVELOPMENT

A major change in the history of firearms began a decade or more before the outbreak of hostilities between North and South. That change was the invention of the self-contained cartridge—powder, detonator, and bullet fashioned into one unit. An early step toward this was the so-called Minnie ball. This was a conical lead bullet made with a hollowed base to contain black powder. Of course, this still required the use of a copper cap to set off the charge. Experiments were being tried, and for a short time paper cartridges were used to contain powder and bullet. These were also unsuccessful. The pinfire cartridge was developed, which had the advantage of eliminating the need for an external percussion cap because a tiny pin projected vertically from the base of a metallic cartridge. The falling hammer struck this pin that hit an internal detonator, igniting the powder. Finally, brass and copper cartridge cases

were designed—small cylindrical cups with the percussion charge imbedded in the base, the powder inside, and the lead bullet crimped to the open end of the shell. This is basically the way cartridges are still made today.

In the 1850s, one of Samuel Colt's own workmen in the Hartford factory, Rollin White, had been experimenting on his own with scrap percussion cylinders and cut off the back of one to facilitate the loading of cartridges from the rear. Even though it was a very simple design that anyone could have thought of, he managed to secure a patent on this bored-through cylinder in 1855. (A patent had been issued in France a year earlier to Eugene Lefaucheux for this same bored-through cylinder. The pistol he produced used a pinfire cartridge.) In the United States, Rollin White offered to sell the rights to his employer, Samuel Colt, who turned it down because Colt was still manufacturing only percussion

Often, L'Amour depicted his heroes as being excellent revolver shots. They were not marksmen in the usual sense of shooting at a target with the arm extended and sighting down the barrel. These were men who, by natural ability or long practice, could fire from a low angle, triangulating from eye to target to pistol, and hit what they aimed at.

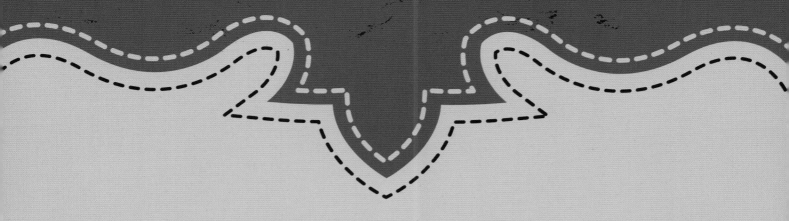

revolvers. White then took his cylinder to Smith & Wesson who paid him to use the bored-through cylinder to accommodate their cartridge weapons.

When Samuel Colt belatedly saw the advantage of cartridge revolvers, he was stymied from making them because White now owned a patent on the design and had sold the manufacturing rights to a competing firm, Smith & Wesson, who forged ahead with the new cartridge revolvers in the decade preceding the Civil War.

During the time that White owned the patent, he was forced to spend a good deal of his profits suing other firms for patent infringement.

Even after the invention of the self-contained metallic cartridge, black powder remained in use until a new smokeless powder was developed in France in 1885. As long as black gunpowder was the only propellant, shooting from hiding was difficult since each shot blew out a cloud of whitish smoke that betrayed the shooter's position. In L'Amour's novel *Kilrone,* a handful of men and women were cooped up in an adobe building trying to hold off a massive Indian attack. The acrid gunpowder smoke from constant firing filled the confined space to such a degree they could not see each other and had to get down on the floor to breathe.

Remington, throughout its history, made both handguns and long guns. (After the Civil War, orders for weapons dropped off severely. In order to stay in business, Remington agreed to manufacture a new invention—the typewriter.)

Innovator though he was, Samuel Colt was slow to pick up on the advanced technology of the metallic cartridge.

He had become famous by inventing and patenting, in the 1830s, the rotating cylinder that would fire five or more consecutive shots without reloading. His first commercial pistol in 1836 was known as the Patterson, named after the New Jersey town where it was manufactured. It had a spur trigger, .36 caliber and five chambers in the cylinder. For lack of a sufficient market, the Colt company fell on hard times and went out of business. But later, Sam Colt's persistence was the spark that reignited the company. Back on their feet again, Colt, with the help of a man named Walker, designed and built the so-called Walker Colt in 1847. This was the gun that helped Colt make its reputation when Sam equipped a company of Texas Rangers with them. This new six-shot .44 more than evened the odds with the hostile Indians on the Texas plains. From that nine-pound Walker, Colt moved

These two guns are single-shot black powder, percussion cap muzzleloaders that date from approximately 1820 up to the Civil War. After the war they would have been obsolete when cartridge weapon repeaters came into general use. The pistol has a detachable stock so it could be fired from the shoulder. These detachable stocks were made during the Civil War for Colt revolvers as well, but were not popular and the idea of detachable shoulder stocks was dropped within a few years. Guns like these were in use during the fur trapper, mountain man period of the 1830s and 1840s. Robert Redford used a Pennsylvania-made Hawken brand rifle very much like this one in the movie *Jeremiah Johnson.*

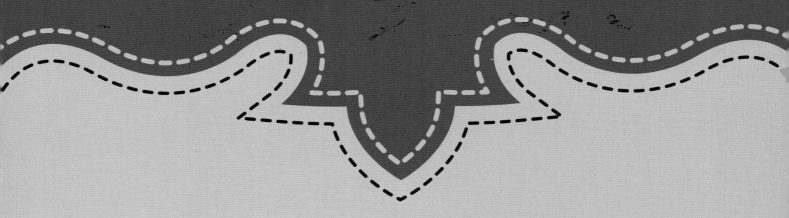

L'Amour's peace officers were typically not depicted as lightning-fast gunfighters. Most had no need to be since they had the force of law to back them when disarming drunks, rowdy cowboys, or troublemakers, and seldom needed to engage in shootouts.

on to manufacture the slightly smaller Dragoon pistol. The revolver was evolving and being improved. Shortly after came the Colt .36 Navy of 1851 and the Colt 1860 Army .44, both of which were widely used during the Civil War. These were all finely wrought, single-action percussion revolvers, graceful, well-balanced and easy to use. Sam even established a factory in London to keep up with demand.

Strangely enough, Colt's all-time best-selling handgun of the percussion era was not the big-bore, heavy revolver, but rather the 1848–1849 .31 caliber pocket pistol. It weighed only about 23 ounces and was small enough to fit into a pocket or reticule, or be tucked under a belt. Until it was discontinued in the early 1880s, Colt sold approximately 335,000 of these small guns. Convenient as a self-defense weapon, this little five-shot pistol was carried to the gold fields of California, was ordered by Wells Fargo for its stage drivers and railroad express messengers, and was a backup weapon for gamblers, bartenders, storekeepers, and

thousands of ordinary citizens who wanted the security of personal protection but didn't need a heavy hunk of iron dragging at the hip.

Even though his major competitors, Smith & Wesson and Remington, quickly adopted the use of cartridges, Colt was reluctant to change (similar to Henry Ford hanging onto the proven Model T long after automobile design had moved on). The so-called "King of Pistoleers," Wild Bill Hickok, never changed either, and continued to use his fancy, but obsolete, twin percussion Navy Colts until an assassin in Deadwood murdered him in 1876.

Samuel Colt died in 1862, and it wasn't until the White patent expired in 1869 that the Colt company was finally able to begin making cartridge guns and catching up with the competition. Nevertheless, catch up they did. With their 1873 model Colt .45, dubbed the "Peacemaker," they took the lead and never looked back. This single-action revolver became the standard weapon on the frontier for the rest of the century and was dubbed "the gun that won the West." It is the sidearm that is most described in novels and most seen in western movies to this day. In the 1870s and 1880s, an unadorned, blued model of the Peacemaker with wooden grips could be had for $15—a reasonable price for the time. But this represented half a month's wages for an ordinary cowhand. This gun was also known as the Single Action Army (SAA) because the model with the 7 ½-inch barrel was bought in large quantities by the government to arm the troops on the frontier.

In the history of the American West, Colt and Winchester were by far the most famous and widely used of any makes of firearms. For years, each company manufactured and sold both pistols and rifles. Around the turn of the twentieth century, they decided not to compete, and thereafter Colt made only revolvers, and Winchester only rifles. Before they stopped competing, Colt produced a rifle with a revolving cylinder and also a pump-action rifle they named the Lightning.

During his lifetime, Samuel Colt had also opposed making a double-action revolver (where one motion of squeezing the trigger cocked the hammer, rotated the cylinder, and tripped the hammer, firing the gun). Colt felt there was no need for such a complex mechanism, and the effort of pulling

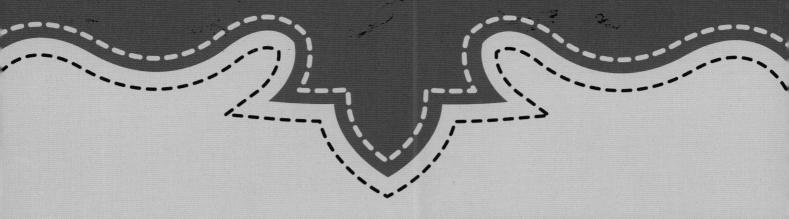

the trigger would throw off the shooter's aim. When the Colt firm finally got around to making a double action, it was the 1877 Lightning, a .38 caliber. (The same gun in .41 caliber was known as the Thunderer.) Both had bird's head-shaped grips. Sam may have been more correct than he knew because the complicated workings of this first model drove many a gunsmith to distraction trying to repair, adjust, and keep them in working order. The following year, Colt came out with another double action, the Frontier revolver, in a larger caliber with a longer barrel, but featuring the same bird's head grip. It, along with later double-action models, were much improved and their mechanisms held up to hard usage.

LESS FAMOUS COMPETITORS

Colt and Winchester, while leaders in their field, were not the only guns used in the West. Dozens of other brands of weaponry showed up on the frontier, and they weren't all new. Many of those who brought their Civil War percussion revolvers with them paid a gunsmith to convert them to fire cartridges. The Colt and Remington factories actually did a good business converting their own guns. After conversion, the pistol retained the same general appearance—Colts with the open top frame (no metal across the top of the cylinder), but there were no nipples for percussion caps, and the ramming loading lever was removed from under the barrel and replaced with a spring-loaded rod to punch out empty shells. Except for retaining its original solid frame, Remingtons sported the same changes.

The famous Derringer was a one- or two-shot pistol, often of heavy caliber, similar to the one used by John Wilkes Booth to murder President Abraham Lincoln. Many brands of similar small guns flooded the market. These were short-range hideout guns that carried a lethal punch and were often carried by gamblers or women.

One of the best-made handguns of the last quarter of the nineteenth century was the Merwin-Hulbert. The design, tight tolerances, fit, and finish of these guns were outstanding. Many were turned out from the factory nickel-plated

An 1889 Model 95, Type II Model 3 Double Derringer lays across the tools of the Old West gambling trade. These short-range hideout guns carried a lethal punch and were often carried by gamblers or women.

and sporting pearl or ivory grips. The whole cylinder and barrel assembly pulled forward and turned slightly to load, or to expel empties. Barrel lengths could be switched at will. But the Merwin-Hulbert never gained the popularity of the top three makes, even though they made pocket pistols and larger holster models in a variety of calibers up to .44. L'Amour did not mention any of his protagonists using one of these, but he did have a character in *Lando* use a handgun that was even less known—a Walch Navy pistol. Invented in 1859, it was a cap and ball revolver that used two shots per cylinder and had two triggers.

Many other makes of weapons were used on the frontier, including long guns such as the Ballard, Whitney, Burgess, and the high-quality Marlin rifles. Manhattan revolvers, the Pettengill double-action hammerless, the Massachusetts Arms copy of the British Adams, the Hopkins and Allen pocket pistol, and the Starr were only a few of the others. And the history of the West would not be complete without

Heavily armed guards aboard a stagecoach prepare for another trip. To say that their lives depended on their shooting skills and the performance of their guns and ammo is a bit of an understatement.

mentioning the Sharps, a single-shot .50-caliber shoulder arm that was often used as a long-range buffalo gun.

The trapdoor Springfield carbine, another single-shot rifle, was carried by mounted cavalry. For fear of soldiers wasting costly ammunition, the US Government did not adopt a repeating rifle for its troops until selecting the bolt action Krag-Jorgenson during the Spanish-American War of 1898.

Several makes of double and single barrel shotguns were also available in a variety of sizes. Scatter guns had a multitude of uses aside from being used to hunt game birds. Stagecoach guards and bartenders used them for protection from violent or rowdy patrons, and they were also used by lawmen who wanted a short-range weapon capable of doing maximum damage.

In effect, the sodbuster, rancher, cowboy, businessman, saloonkeeper, railroad express messenger, lawman, and criminal had a wide variety of weaponry available to choose from during that ever-changing block of time and space that was the American Western frontier between the Civil War and the turn of the century.

Some of L'Amour's characters carried and used one of the more popular handguns, a Smith & Wesson Russian model (almost the same as the American model). This was a .44 top break single action revolver that had many adherents, including Jesse James.

Of course, there was always the odd style of gun that turned up now and then, such as the LeMat, a 9-shot percussion revolver that could also fire a shotgun shell in a lower barrel. (A LeMat was used by the hero in the movie *Cold Mountain*.) In spite of its name, a New Orleans doctor invented this gun and a few early ones were made in Philadelphia before manufacturing was switched to France.

Above: The Dodge City Peace Commissioners of 1883 included Bat Masterson (back row, third from the left) and Wyatt Earp (front row, second from the left). Earp left Dodge City in 1878 and settled in Tombstone where he acquired the gambling concession at the Oriental Saloon and his brother Virgil became town marshal. Brother Morgan worked for the local police department. **Left:** Very rarely in the real West did these gunfighters call one another out to stalk down the middle of a dirt street at high noon and test their fast-draw abilities.

One of the few remaining artifacts of Billy the Kid's life is a 2x3-inch ferrotype taken by an unknown photographer sometime in late 1879 or early 1880. It is the only image of William McCarty (his real name) that scholars agree is authentic. It sold at auction in 2011 for $2.3 million and is the ninth most expensive photograph ever sold.

continued from page 49

Finally, the 1873 model Winchester became the standard, center-fire rifle that rose above all other long guns in popularity, just as the 1873 Colt Peacemaker became the standard revolver. L'Amour mentioned the common practice of using the same interchangeable ammunition for both of these weapons when a man carried the Colt on his hip and the Winchester in a saddle scabbard.

Another type of repeating rifle in fairly wide use during and after the war was the Spencer. Men on horseback, for ease of handling, often used the shorter carbine model. This gun fired a large .56 caliber bullet. A flexible loading tube was extracted from the butt of the stock, the bullets inserted and the tube pushed back inside and locked into place. The loading lever was made into the trigger guard, but the hammer on this one had to be cocked by hand. Clint Eastwood used one of these in his movie, *Unforgiven*.

Apparently assuming that his readers were familiar with these weapons, L'Amour did not go into detailed descriptions when he wrote about his characters using them. He normally simply referred to them as a Spencer, Colt, or Winchester.

Often L'Amour depicted his heroes as being excellent revolver shots. They were not marksmen in the usual sense of shooting at a target with the arm extended and sighting down the barrel. These were men who, by natural ability or long practice, could fire from a low angle, triangulating from eye to target to pistol, and hit what they aimed at. These were the fast-draw gunfighters who have become a cliché in western books and movies. Very rarely in the real West did these gunfighters call one another out to stalk down the middle of a dirt street at high noon and test their fast-draw abilities. Although L'Amour did describe men who considered themselves very fast with a gun going up against each other in climactic scenes, he usually depicted antagonists acting and reacting in normal situations created as the story unfolded— in stage stations, saloons, cabins, ambushes in the dark near a campfire, mountain caves, or sudden encounters on horseback. In addition, many of his main characters were also excellent shots with a rifle. Not only did the hero have these skills, but very often the villain did as well, setting up the tension of an eventual showdown.

Unless they had an unusual past, L'Amour's peace officers were just that—those employed to keep the peace. They were not depicted as lightning-fast gunfighters. Most had no need to be since they had the force of law to back them when

On October 5, 1892, the Dalton Gang planned a double bank robbery in their hometown of Coffeyville, Kansas. After a fierce shootout with a group of armed citizens led by Marshall Charles Connelly, nearly the entire gang was killed, along with Connelly and three citizens. The handcuffed bodies of the gang were laid out like trophies in front of the Coffeyville Jail. From left to right are Bill Powers, Bob Dalton, Grat Dalton, and Dick Broadwell. Youngest brother Emmett Dalton was badly wounded but survived.

disarming drunks, rowdy cowboys, or troublemakers, and seldom needed to engage in shootouts. In *North to the Rails,* L'Amour wrote, "For six years he ran the town, and kept it free of serious trouble. He rarely had to draw his gun, and several times he held his fire to give the other man a chance to drop his, and they usually did—all but one.

"That man elected to fire . . . and missed. Borden Chantry did not miss.

"That was the shooting that led to his death, for the men who came up the trail to kill him were friends of the dead man, and they staged the ambush that wiped out Borden Chantry."

In the authentic West, strength of character and personality, courage to face trouble, and skill with a gun were very often traits shared by both outlaws and lawmen, whether the peacekeepers were deputy marshals with federal appointments or elected sheriffs. In actuality, history records numerous men who spent time on both sides of the law, switching from one side to the other at will. One man who worked both sides at once was Henry Plummer. Outwardly, he was the sheriff of Bannack, Montana, but secretly headed up a gang of road agents. He was eventually caught by vigilantes and hanged.

Above: Incredibly, this home outside Kearny, Missouri, where Jesse James was reared, is still standing today. This is how the homestead appeared in 1877, several years before Jesse was killed. The James brothers became a staple in dime novels of the era, peaking in the 1880s following Jesse's death. James has often been used as a fictional character in many western novels, including some published while he was alive. **Right:** With a $10,000 price on his head, fellow gang members Charley and Robert Ford betrayed Jesse James in April 1882, shooting and killing him at age thirty-four inside his St. Joseph, Missouri, home. At the time of the shooting, Jesse hardly ever took off his guns and never turned his back to a door or window if he could help it.

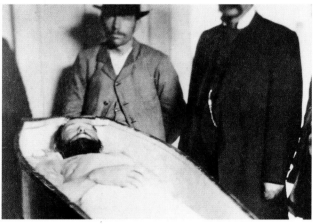

Brothers Bob, Grat, and Emmett Dalton had been deputy US marshals in the Oklahoma Territory before turning outlaw in 1890. The Dalton gang decided to make history by robbing two banks at the same time in the town of Coffeyville, Kansas, in October 1892. But they ran into a buzz saw of irate citizens. Bob, Grat, and two other gang members were shot down on the streets within minutes. Badly wounded, only Emmett Dalton survived the gang's disastrous robbery attempt.

After recovering, he spent many years in prison and later became an honest, law-abiding citizen, giving lectures on avoiding the evils of crime.

Anyone who had what it took to tame a lawless Kansas cowtown, for example, also had what it took—if he had no scruples—to make a career in the more lucrative, dangerous field of armed robbery. Sometimes city fathers compromised their principles by hiring the toughest man they could find to wear the badge, be he saint or sinner.

Above and right: L'Amour, himself, claimed a connection to the Old West by having met several former lawmen who had been alive and active when the Wild West was still in the process of being tamed and settled. Two of the three more famous and long-lived of these western lawmen were Chris Madsen and Bill Tilghman. Heck Thomas was the third.
Lower right: The caption under this apparently arranged turn-of-the-century photograph simply reads "Gone Over the Big Divide." Though violence was certainly present in the Old West, most historians would argue that it wasn't nearly as prevalent as the dime novels, pulp magazines, and movies and television would suggest.

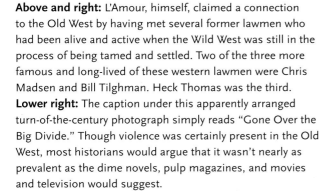

They reasoned you had to gamble by fighting fire with fire, and let the law-abiding citizens stay out of the way.

But, as seen in Coffeyville, citizens didn't always stay out of the way. In *Hanging Woman Creek,* L'Amour made reference to another historic incident when an irate group of armed townspeople shot up the James/Younger gang who rode north from their native Missouri to rob the bank in the quiet town of Northfield, Minnesota. Some gang members were killed, others were captured, but Jesse managed to escape and continued on the outlaw trail for another six years.

L'Amour, himself, claimed a connection to the Old West by having met several former lawmen who had been alive and active when the Wild West was still in the process of being tamed and settled. Two of the three more famous and long-lived of these western lawmen were Chris Madsen and Bill Tilghman. Heck Thomas was the third. These men came to be known as The Three Guardsmen because they were prominent in capturing over

300 outlaws in the Oklahoma Territory over several years, killing several of them.

Chris Madsen (Rormose) dropped his last name when he emigrated to the United States from Denmark in 1876. He claimed to have previously served in the Danish army and then for

Above: Any Old West outlaws meeting a group of heavily armed Texas Rangers like this would certainly be in for a battle. Posse groups were common in the wide-open spaces of the frontier where many an outlaw would attempt an escape. **Opposite:** From their earliest days, the Texas Rangers were surrounded with the mystique of the Old West. Although popular culture's image of the Rangers is typically one of rough living, tough talk, and a quick draw, Ranger Captain John "Rip" Ford described the men who served him thus: "A large proportion…were unmarried. A few of them drank intoxicating liquors. Still, it was a company of sober and brave men. They knew their duty and they did it. While in a town they made no braggadocio demonstration. They did not gallop through the streets, shoot, and yell. They had a specie of moral discipline, which developed moral courage. They did right because it was right."

several years in the French Foreign Legion. Madsen enlisted in the Fifth Cavalry and served for fifteen years. In 1898 he joined Teddy Roosevelt's Rough Riders. He was a deputy marshal in the Oklahoma Territory, serving in the jurisdiction of Judge Isaac Parker, known as "The Hanging Judge" who held court at Fort Smith, Arkansas, just across the river from the Oklahoma Territory.

L'Amour stated that before he went overseas during World War II, he met and talked to Madsen several times. L'Amour wrote that Madsen had been present when Buffalo Bill Cody had killed the Indian, Yellow Hand, in hand-to-hand combat. When L'Amour met Madsen, he was a deputy US marshal. A solid, stocky man, Madsen lived to be over ninety years of age.

Bill Tilghman was, according to people who knew him, a real gentleman. From Fort Dodge, Iowa, his family moved to Kansas when he was just a child. At the age of sixteen he became a buffalo hunter and kept at this for five years. Although he did not drink, he used the money he saved to buy a saloon in Dodge City. Later he served on a Peace Commission with Wyatt and Virgil Earp, Luke Short, and Bat Masterson, and was an acquaintance of Doc Holliday. He was well respected by everyone as a brave and upright man. Masterson hired him to serve as a deputy sheriff in 1878, and Tilghman remained in law enforcement for most of the rest of his life. In 1889 he moved to Guthrie, Oklahoma, and served for several years as a deputy US marshal, helping clean up the Oklahoma Territory. His reputation was enhanced when he captured the notorious Bill Doolin. The lawman was even elected to the Oklahoma state senate in 1910.

At the age of seventy he was talked into coming out of retirement to serve as a city marshal at

Mannie Hyman's Saloon in Leadville, Colorado, was the final hangout for dentist, gambler, gunfighter, and lawman John "Doc" Holliday. Apparently even he expected an eventual violent death, since his final words were "This is funny" as tuberculosis and alcoholism claimed him in 1877.

Cromwell, Oklahoma. Those who hired him felt that Tilghman, even at an advanced age, still had the reputation and was man enough to help intimidate the lawless element in the 1920s oil boomtowns of Oklahoma. He died on duty. A drunken and corrupt prohibition agent, Wiley Lynn, had been releasing prisoners that Tilghman arrested and the two had words over this. On November 1, 1924, Lynn threatened Tilghman with a gun outside a restaurant. Tilghman attempted to arrest him. In the struggle that followed, Lynn pulled a hideout gun and shot Tilghman twice, killing him.

L'Amour did not give the details of how he happened to meet Bill Tilghman. It is possible they met in Oklahoma where Tilghman lived and where Louis' family moved sometime after they left North Dakota in late 1923. The future author could have been no more than sixteen at the time.

Henry Anderson (Heck) Thomas was the third of The Three Guardsmen. Originally from Georgia, he was only twelve years old when he tagged along with his uncle to a Civil War battle in Virginia. He would find himself in the right place at the right time for a historical moment. During the battle of

A contemporary photograph of the historic OK Corral in Tombstone, Arizona. In actuality, the gunfight did not take place within the OK Corral but in a narrow lot next to Fly's Photographic Studio, six doors west of the rear entrance to the OK Corral on Fremont Street. The two opposing parties were initially only about six feet apart. About thirty shots were fired in thirty seconds. Today, visitors to Tombstone will find figures of the gunfighters at the site where the shootout took place.

Sharpsburg, General Robert E. Lee sent an order back from the front lines to have Union General Phil Kearny's horse brought up so it could be delivered to the general's widow. Young Thomas proudly took the black horse with its saddle and gear forward and handed him over to the general. Even though Heck Thomas went on to an exciting career as a deputy US marshal, he would always consider this boyhood incident one of the highlights of his life. He died of natural causes in 1912 in Oklahoma.

L'Amour never met him, but did meet a number of other less famous lawmen who had survived the early days and were able to tell the young man of many happenings which he later turned into novels. He could even base the physical descriptions and personalities of his fictitious sheriffs and marshals on some of these former lawmen. L'Amour observed, correctly, that he was the last generation who would be able to interview living links with the historic past of the American frontier.

CHAPTER 4

MINING AND RANCHING

L'Amour came along a generation or more after the trail drives and the big mining booms. But he met numerous oldsters in their 70s and 80s who, as young men, had taken part in the settling of the West and gave L'Amour their recollections and firsthand accounts of what it was like.

Even discounting a bit for exaggeration, bragging, and faulty memories that sometimes creep into stories told by old-timers, it was still a living history lesson for L'Amour. Paying close attention to their tales provided him with a great source of material for his novels. Adding extensive reading of journal accounts that were recorded at the time

Below: Gold Rush prospectors on their way to the Klondike stick close together while fording an ice-cold stream. **Opposite:** A group of prospectors pose with their equipment and a heavily laden horse as they prepare for a trip somewhere in the Northwest in 1867.

This incredible 1898 photo seems to be right out of a Cecil B. DeMille epic as an endless line of miners bound for the Klondike gold fields climb over Chilkoot Pass, a high mountain pass through the Boundary Ranges of the Coast Mountains in Alaska and British Columbia.

Above: Riding, roping, and flying hooves are the ways of the cowboy, and for those who still partake in the undertaking of moving animals on horseback, it's virtually unchanged from the way it was in the late 1800s. **Right:** L'Amour apparently was never a working cowboy but did perform manual labor on ranches and farms. One of his more odious jobs was skinning dead cattle to save their hides for making leather.

of the events by pioneers, cowboys, and miners gave him much more. Then, his own rough experiences as a laborer and exploration of the countryside rounded out what he needed to create the adventure stories he put into his books.

L'Amour apparently was never a working cowboy but did manual labor on ranches and farms. One of his more odious jobs was the skinning of dead cattle to save their hides for making leather. But he was around herds and cattle ranchers and the shipping of livestock by rail cars. He knew how brands were used (and altered), and about the care and feeding of livestock, as well as their treatment for various diseases. After all, his father was a veterinarian. The open range had long since been fenced when he came along, and the buffalo were gone, but there was plenty of history of the early days of cattle drives, the Texas longhorns, the fencing, the sheepmen versus the cattlemen, and the range wars of the late 1800s, so that he

4357. "We have It Rich." - Washing and panning gold, Rockerville, Dak. Old: timers, Spriggs, Lamb and Dillon at work. Photo and copyright by Grabill, 1889.

Above: This astonishing 1889 character study proves that some Old West prospectors really do look the way they're sometimes described in western novels and pulp magazines. This photograph was taken in what was then known as the Dakota Territory (North and South Dakota both became states later that same year on November 2). **Left:** This 1889 albumen print immortalizes prospector Archie Smith on the porch of his humble cabin on the shore of Eagle Creek near Murray, Idaho.

was never lacking for information he could use in his books. Several of his early novels dealt with ranching, and often his heroes dreamed of making enough money, legally or by luck, to someday buy a small ranch and start a herd. In his novel *Lando,* part of which took place on the Texas Gulf Coast, his characters briefly met the founder and owner of the famous King Ranch. Richard King was the wealthy rancher who had helped develop the well-known strain of beef cattle known as *Santa Gertrudis.*

In the same novel, L'Amour's characters used a trick to carry several sacks of gold, undetected, past their enemies. The gold had been retrieved from a ship that had foundered on a sand bar off the Texas Gulf Coast. Tying the small sacks together by their tops, they hung the sacks over the backs of steers and then drove the packed herd north and west at night.

One of the many types of short-term jobs L'Amour performed as a young man was doing assessment work on mining claims. Over the past 150 years, mining laws have been passed, amended, and amended again. Mineral rights have varied and become more and more complex. A good example of the laws regarding mining claims took place over two or three decades beginning in the early 1860s during the great silver mining boom near Virginia City, Nevada. L'Amour used this boom as the setting of one of his longer novels, *The Comstock Lode.*

Shares of mining stock and actual deeds to claims were bought and sold by the thousands. Speculation was rampant, and everyone from saloon girls and newspaper editors to hotel owners and mine superintendents bought and sold gilt-edged certificates, hoping they represented underground mineral wealth. One of the provisions of an early mining law allowed a prospector, if he struck a vein of rich ore, to follow that vein wherever it led, even if it intruded into or beneath another man's mine. Over the months and years,

when geology was still a developing science, this led to all kinds of litigation until hundreds of conflicting claims gridlocked the legal system. Over time, many of these lawsuits were abandoned rather than being resolved, especially as pay dirt in the richer mines dwindled out and mines flooded.

Laws regarding placer claims (surface mining) were not terribly difficult to administer. But for those who held lode claims (underground mining), it was a different story. Prospectors who had staked a claim or two and had hopes, but no color, or perhaps very little promising gold, copper, or silver ore, had to hold onto their claims until they could develop them further. One of the provisions of the law stated that a claim was considered to be abandoned and available to anyone else to grab if a certain amount of "assessment" work was not performed on the claim every year, or possibly every six months. This was at least $100 worth of work, or perhaps, depending on the state or territory, a certain number of actual days of work.

L'Amour came along at the very end of the great mining booms, but enough claims were still being worked that he had no trouble during the 1920s finding jobs doing this kind of assessment work. Claim owners who maybe had no high hopes of striking it rich, but still wanted to hold onto their claims just in case, hired others, L'Amour included,

Top: Mine shacks, shafts, carts, and factories were abandoned by the thousands after their short and busy lives came to an end. Because they were often located in remote lands that have never been utilized for anything else, many relics from the mining boom continue to dot the countryside. **Above left:** A hand-colored woodcut of a nineteenth-century illustration portrays prospectors traveling a rough road to the gold regions of California. These were the men known as "The 49ers," named for the year when California was opened up after gold was first discovered at Sutter's Mill the year before. **Above right:** The view inside an abandoned mine in the Nevada desert. One of the provisions of an early mining law allowed a prospector, if he struck a vein of rich ore, to follow that vein wherever it led, even if it intruded into or beneath another man's mine.

to do the minimum amount of assessment work on their claims to legally keep possession of them.

This work varied by the claim, but L'Amour stated he learned to use a single jack. Single jacking was actually holding what amounted to a long, sharp chisel with one hand and pounding it with a heavy hammer. It was usually done to hand drill a hole in hard rock where a stick of dynamite could be placed to blast loose a large amount of rock at once. Double jacking was the same thing, but this required two men—one to hold the drill (like a long, pointed chisel) while a second man hit it with a sledgehammer. The one with the hammer had to be good, or risk smashing the holder's hands. L'Amour said that by the time he came along, steam drills had replaced single and double jacking. Assessment work might be nothing more complex than digging, shoveling, and hauling out rock and dirt from the head of a drift (the dead end of a working tunnel)—back-breaking labor to be sure, but not dangerous unless performed inside an unstable mine shaft, or one with poison gas.

Just after Lee and Grant formally ended the war at the Appomattox Courthouse in April 1865, thousands of fighting men, both North and South, straggled home to take up farming once again, planting crops and thinking about raising livestock

Below: An 1867 photo of the Gold Hill mining camp in California gives one a good view of what these hastily built (albeit by hand!) settlements actually looked like.

Above: The final destinations for western beef were the immense stockyards of the East. This 1890's scene is the Union Stockyards in Chicago. In 1906 this stockyard would become the catalyst for the formation of the first federal food regulations following the publication of Upton Sinclair's novel *The Jungle*, which detailed the deplorable conditions in the meat packing industry.

Left: Trail drivers in the late 1800s had to contend with all kinds of obstacles—tick fever, hail, stampede-causing lightning, Indians, rustlers, lack of water, flooding rivers, cattle losing weight on the trail, and others trying to get started in business picking off unbranded calves or strays. Ranching was a difficult and dangerous occupation, and it required money and courage to get started.

as many had done before they went off to fight. In the many months it took for those who produced the food to reestablish themselves, there was a shortage in the eastern half of the country.

A few enterprising individuals saw the meat-hunger in the East as an opportunity. The plains and hill country of Texas was home to thousands of wild longhorn cattle, there for the taking. A fortune could be made. All they had to do was round up herds of these vicious wild animals and somehow get them to the slaughterhouses in Chicago and Omaha. Easier said than done. These muscular, rangy cattle with the long, sharp horns had been running wild in the brush for years and weren't about to submit to being captured. Also, their meat was tough and stringy. But they represented food for millions—if they could be brought to market.

A horse thief is hanged without trial by two cowboys and left to die in this 1916 illustration. Frontier justice placed cattle rustling and horse thievery right up there with murder.

With courage, hard work, and luck, it could be done. And some did. For the next twenty years, cattle ranching in the West grew and grew to become a huge business. The traditions of the cowboy and the cattle drive were born.

Not only did some hardy men capture and drive these longhorns to market but, over time, began to interbreed them with stockier shorthorns that produced better beef. The trouble was, how were they to get these longhorns to a population hungry for beef? Soon after the war railroads began building west, transforming American life and commerce. Ranchers on the southern plains held periodic roundups and hired cowboys to work for weeks, driving herds of several hundred to several thousand cattle north to the railheads for shipment east to market. At first the wild Texas cattle had to be dehorned to allow them to be loaded into the stock cars without injuring each other since many of their horns had a span of several feet.

Trail drivers had to contend with all kinds of obstacles—tick fever, hail, stampede-causing lightning, Indians, rustlers, lack of water, flooding rivers, cattle losing weight on the trail, and others trying to get started in business picking off unbranded calves or strays. Ranching was a difficult and dangerous occupation, and it required money and courage to get started.

This whole enterprise stretched over a generation or more and provided fertile material for all kinds of stories. Many western novelists—including L'Amour—set fictional tales around the cattle industry—raising, herding, breeding, men fighting over water rights and land, rustling and altering brands, Indians picking off beeves to eat in place of the vanished buffalo. A good example of a L'Amour novel set around a cattle drive was *North to the Rails* that takes place mostly in Colorado.

The practice of picking up and keeping unbranded calves and strays from a neighbor's land—some called it rustling—was the cause of one of the most infamous feuds in the early West.

Above: Cattle ranching provided L'Amour with fertile material for all kinds of stories: raising, herding, breeding, cattle drives, men fighting over water rights and land, rustling and altering brands, and Indians picking off beeves to eat in place of the vanished buffalo. **Right:** This hand-colored woodcut captures a cattlemen's raid on a sheepherders' camp in Colorado during the livestock range wars of the late 1800s. Prejudice against the recently arrived sheepherders, and battles over land and water rights, fueled the confrontations.

This was the Graham-Tewksbury feud south of Arizona's Mogollon Rim. It started in 1887 and lasted until 1892 and became known to history as the Pleasant Valley War. Before it was over, five of six brothers of both families had been killed, and the one survivor had moved away and sold his land. Many others were wounded. During one siege of a ranch house, the dead body of a man just killed lay in the yard and was eaten by hogs because it was too dangerous for his family to retrieve the body. In the midst of all this, when the gunfighting and bushwhacking got so bad that the law from the territorial capitol at Prescott could not deal with it, a group of vigilantes was formed and swept through the valley. Even those who were merely suspected of wrongdoing—rustling, thievery, or intended murder—were rounded up and routinely lynched. Even some innocent travelers were

Wealthy and powerful cattle barons resented the sheepherders who came later with their flocks in the late 1800s. Pictured is a Navajo women tending her flock in Utah's Monument Valley in the 1960s.

Above: The invention of barbed wire was one of the major causes of the decline of the cattle drive era in the West. Once boundaries became established on the open range, troubles began, and the free land required for big cattle drives to be successful was gone. **Opposite:** Another event that proved the end of the cattle barons in the Great Plains was the long, severe winter of 1886–1887. In the extreme cold and snow where most migrating buffalo herds could probably have survived, the blizzards killed off thousands of cattle, and many ranchers lost their entire herds.

known to have died this way. There was something about the sight of maggot-ridden bodies hanging from trees that had a quieting effect on lawlessness that no amount of gunfire could accomplish.

In the cattle ranching industry, a number of ranchers were well off and influential. One of the best known and respected ranchers was Montana's Granville Stuart, who appeared as a minor character in L'Amour's *Hanging Woman Creek*.

Another rancher from Texas, who lived to be over ninety years old, became a legend. He was Charles Goodnight. One of the first to take up cattle ranching, he and his partner Oliver Loving, pioneered what became known as the Goodnight-Loving Trail when they scouted a route west into southern New Mexico and then north through

Colorado to Cheyenne. Others followed their trail. In time, at least three or four more major trails were laid out.

When the spiking of railroad tracks had not yet progressed into the Great Plains, the Shawnee Trail curved east and north to Kansas City and Sedalia, Missouri. Later, the Western Trail went almost due north from Brownsville and San Antonio to Kearny, Nebraska. One of the most widely used was the Chisholm Trail from Waco through Kansas into Nebraska. As the building of the railroads progressed west, the railheads came a little closer—Ellsworth, Hays City, Abilene, Wichita, Dodge City in Kansas and Kearny and Ogallala in Nebraska. Legends of the wild towns and the marshals who tamed them grew up during this

period. The American image of the cowboy was also formed with the cowhands spending weeks on the trail from Texas with herds and then blowing off steam at these railroad towns. Each of these major trails north varied according to the time of year, the size of the herd, weather, and a number of other factors.

A cultural and physical clash began early in this quarter century between 1865 and 1890. And that was the clash between the whites who had come first to graze cattle on the public lands and those who arrived a little later with flocks of sheep to do the same.

Those who had grown rich in the space of a few years raising and selling beef cattle thought of themselves as controlling all the land their herds grazed on, even though everything beyond 160 acres allotted per individual by the Homestead Act of 1862 was public land. These cattle barons, especially those in Wyoming and Montana, were wealthy and powerful. They resented the sheepmen who came later with their flocks. These ranchers and their cowboys circulated false rumors about sheep—that they poisoned the land and the water for cattle, they ruined the grazing by eating the grass down to the roots so that it took another growing season before it would regenerate, that the smell left by flocks caused cattle to shy away from land where sheep had grazed.

Of course all of these allegations turned out to be false. When sheep were spread out to graze and moved from pasture to pasture, they did not eat the grass down to the roots. Their sharp cloven hooves helped till the soil, and their droppings fertilized it. There was no truth to the rumor that they poisoned the water.

But, before all this became common knowledge, prejudice reigned and so did the cattlemen versus sheepmen wars. Often shepherds were foreigners—Basques from Spain—along with Indians, Mexicans, or half-breeds, making them subject to

Future president Theodore Roosevelt moved to North Dakota to become a cattle rancher following the death of his first wife (and his mother only hours earlier) in 1884. During his time in the West he wrote three books—*Hunting Trips of a Ranchman*, *Ranch Life and the Hunting-Trail*, and *The Wilderness Hunter*. Like many other ranchers in the territory, the Blizzard of 1886–1887 wiped out his herd and he returned to New York to begin yet another chapter in his amazing life.

racial taunts as well. Shepherds were threatened if they didn't leave the area. There were incidents of outright murder of sheepmen, in addition to mass shootings and clubbings of their flocks and even their dogs. Sometimes masked nightriders carried out the slaughter. Now and then, deadlines were established by ranchers—borders beyond which sheep were not allowed.

Even Charles Goodnight established a deadline with sheepmen in Texas, and both sides adhered to it peaceably for years. Goodnight ranched in the Panhandle and ran cattle in Palo Duro Canyon not far from the present Amarillo. This mighty gash in the flat Texas plains was a perfect place for cattle since it contained water, trees, and grass, and considerable protection from storms and winter snows.

Goodnight was even credited with devising the design of the chuckwagon. It was such a practical invention that it was copied and widely used on trail drives for decades.

Two things ended the cattle drive era in the West. The first was barbed wire. Because grass was often sparse, vast acreages were needed to support large grazing herds. If a rancher wanted to keep control of his herds and know where his property joined another man's, he would normally put a fence. But because of the lack of trees for rails and fence posts, or stones for boundary walls, or time for hedges to grow, property lines could not be established with any accuracy, nor could cattle be prevented from straying. When they could be erected, ordinary wire fences were easily pushed over by livestock.

A farmer in Illinois named Joseph Glidden patented the first barbed wire in 1874. Thereafter, hundreds of various designs came on the market. Here was a practical solution, and its use spread into the West. Ranchers, accustomed to the traditional open range, resented it and the fact that it cut across established trails and often prevented their herds from getting to water. Fence cutting and armed reprisals became routine. Barbed wire was also used to create deadlines between sheep and cattle. It was illegal to fence public land, and sometimes deputies cut fences as part of their duties, making them very unpopular with ranchers.

The second event that proved the end of the cattle barons in the Great Plains was the long, severe winter of 1886–1887. In the extreme cold and snow where most migrating buffalo herds could probably have survived, the blizzards killed off thousands of cattle, especially those that were fenced and couldn't drift with the wind and possibly find partial shelter in draws or copses of trees. Many ranchers lost their entire herds and were financially ruined. (This was also the storm that wiped out Teddy Roosevelt's herd during his North Dakota ranching days, sending him back to the East Coast). It became known as the "Big Die-Up." Some ranchers even turned to raising sheep because those wooly animals seemed to fare better in cold and snow.

Settlers looked for revenue wherever they could find it, even if it meant setting some trap lines. Note how skinny the hounds are in this detailed study of life in the Old West.

CHAPTER 5

WOMEN

Louis L'Amour depicted women of all kinds in his novels—some willful, some weak and dependent, some quietly strong and stable, some independent, some thirsting for adventure, some who were striving to work as partners alongside their husbands or future husbands and become homemakers, some prostitutes with hearts of gold, some depraved, some vicious and conniving, and even some mentally challenged.

An example of the latter type was seen in the novel *Hanging Woman Creek*. During the story, strange hoof prints were discovered here and there in the snow. They appeared to have been made by a horse with leather horseshoes. Something ominous? Did they belong to some villainous character, or an Indian who would figure into the plot? No. Toward the end of the book, it turned out the tracks were made by a horse ridden by Lottie Orrum, sister of Clyde Orrum, a long-dead outlaw, who is not part of the story. She had been close to her brother, and his death had slightly unhinged her mental faculties. She'd been riding about, taking home-cooked food to people. When she finally came on the scene, Pronto Pike, one of the main characters, talked to her like a loving parent.

Above: A turn of the century stereo card simply entitled "A Girl from the Golden West." L'Amour wrote about all kinds of women, everything from independent to criminal to mentally unstable. **Opposite:** Perhaps one of America's first females to compete directly against men in a male-dominated pastime, sharpshooter Annie Oakley wowed thousands when she began travelling the country with the Buffalo Bill Wild West Show in 1885. Annie began trapping at a young age, and shooting and hunting by age eight to support her siblings and her widowed mother.

Above left: Initial fame settled upon actress Lillie Langtry accidentally, thanks to her great beauty and sense of style. Abundant romantic scandals helped spread her renown. But it was Lillie's own determination, imagination, shrewdness, and independent spirit that cemented her enduring success as an actress and businesswoman throughout most of her life. **Above right:** As one might expect, the Old West offered few career opportunities for single women. One of the more respectable was that of schoolteacher. This teacher is dressed in the period style clothing and is wearing round glasses with a chain. **Opposite:** The women in L'Amour's novels could be good riders and ranchers, but rarely did they handle guns. Typically, most of the females in his novels were described as attractive in one way or another.

He advised her to comb her hair and clean up and take pride in her appearance. Since she liked to cook and was good at it, he advised her to find a job cooking to support herself.

In *The Lonely Men*, L'Amour introduced the reader to Laura Sackett, a very pretty, ladylike young woman who turned out to be conniving, hating, low-down, and vicious. She had married Orrin Sackett, brother of William Tell Sackett, but they were estranged and she was in Tucson while he was in Washington, DC. In order to get back at the Sackett family, especially her husband, she concocted a tale about their (nonexistent) five-year-old son who'd been captured by Apaches and taken into Mexico. She beguiled Tell Sackett into riding across the border to rescue her son, knowing Tell would probably be killed in the attempt. Tell's death would hurt her husband, Orrin, more than anything else she could do to him, in addition to bringing grief to the entire Sackett clan. Even though she didn't die in the end, she was exposed and shamed when her plot failed.

But more typical of the women L'Amour wrote about was Ann Farley, younger sister of Philo Farley, an immigrant to America from Ireland. After her brother traveled to America and settled on a homestead to raise horses in Montana, she came to join him. Barnabas Pike, first-person narrator of this

Above: In 1915, rodeo star Bonnie McCarroll takes a hard landing during the Pendleton (Oregon) Round-Up in this photograph that drew national attention at the time. Fourteen years later while giving a bronc-riding exhibition during the same event, she was thrown from her mount, "Black Cat," and the animal turned a somersault upon her. She was rushed to a hospital but later died of her spinal wounds and pneumonia at age thirty-two. **Right:** In one novel, a very determined woman had been given a cattle ranch by a male relative and was competently running it when the hero came into her life. She and the hero teamed up against a wealthy rancher who was bent on overrunning her land with his large cattle herd, pushing her and the neighbors out. With the help of the lone rider hero, the threat was finally destroyed.

story, met her and was immediately stricken by her beauty, charm, and intelligence. "She was slim and tall, and she had the kind of red hair they call auburn—a lot of it. Her eyes were almost violet and there were a few freckles over her nose." She was a good horsewoman, which Barnabas appreciated. "She was a lady, every inch of her, I could see that, and there was something clean and fine about her that made a man look twice." It turned out she was also brave and resourceful, saving her wounded brother after outlaws who burned their cabin attacked both of them.

Rarely did L'Amour write about a rough, dirty, mannish female such as Calamity Jane. Even those who did not measure up in loyalty and

steadfastness were usually at least attractive. In *Taggart,* hero Adam Stark was married to a beautiful woman, Consuelo. They, along with Adam's sister Miriam, were camped in a canyon in the hills north of Globe, Arizona. Hiding from hostile Apaches, he was taking out a little gold ore each day from a secret mine he'd found, hoping to get enough gold for them to live on when, or if, they could escape the savages in the surrounding hills. During the whole novel, Consuelo (Connie) complained about hating the wilderness solitude. She wanted the luxury of San Francisco. She belittled her husband. For one thing, she considered Adam a weakling because he had backed off from a deadly confrontation with a man in Tucson who'd made advances to Consuelo. She was determined to run off with this man whom she fancied to be much stronger. Miriam, who was a much more stable person, tried to reason with Connie. Miriam, herself, was depicted as the quiet, sensible one,

Above: A very young Mary Katherine "Big Nose Kate" Haroney (seated on left) with her sister Wilhelmina in 1865. This picture was taken close to the time when the girls' parents died and they both became orphans. Later in life, Kate was a companion of Doc Holliday and Wyatt Earp when all three were in Tombstone, and she was present when the OK Corral Shootout took place. She died in 1940 and is buried in Prescott, Arizona.
Left top: A companion of Butch Cassidy and the Sundance Kid, Etta Place remains one of the Old West's biggest enigmas; both her origin and her fate remain shrouded in mystery. Those who had met Place claimed the first thing they noticed about her was that she was strikingly pretty, cordial, refined, and an excellent shot with a rifle. **Left bottom:** Belle Starr was a western outlaw whose exploits were made famous in dime novels soon after her mysterious murder at age forty-one in 1889. She was married numerous times, spent nine months in prison in Detroit, and at one time was part of the James-Younger Gang, many members of which were childhood friends of hers.

Above: Authentic old cabins are lit up against the darkening sky at 4 Eagle Ranch in Wolcott, Colorado. These are the type of buildings many frontier women would manage for their families. **Right:** Some of the female characters in L'Amour novels were downright depraved, and others vicious and conniving. In the 1890s, Laura Bullion was a member of Butch Cassidy's gang, the Wild Bunch, and had a colorful career before and after that time. Bullion should not be confused with the mysterious Etta Place, girlfriend to Wild Bunch gang member the Sundance Kid. The Sundance Kid was killed in Bolivia. Laura died in 1961 at age 85.

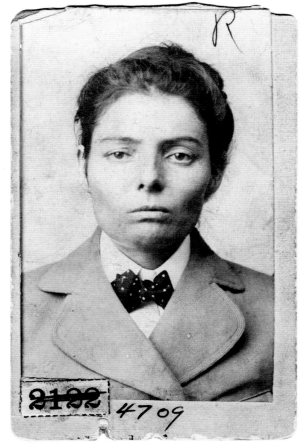

less impetuous and more discerning about what she wanted in a man.

In the end, after Adam took care of the villain, Consuelo belatedly realized the strength of her husband, and how the man she'd been attracted to was actually the coward. And Miriam, the steady, careful one, gradually fell in love with the lone rider, Taggart, who had come to the aid of all three of them earlier in the story.

Older women and mothers were nearly always depicted as wise and nurturing. They had reared families and seen their children to adulthood

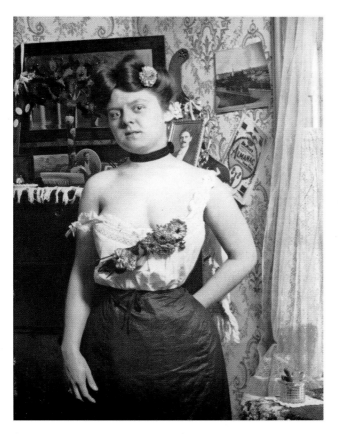

What's a western without a mention of brothels, madams, and prostitutes? L'Amour never shied away from that aspect of the Old West, although he certainly refrained from describing any details of the actual business that took place.

through years of toil and sacrifice. Such were the mothers in the Sackett clan, although most were only remembered with fondness and didn't appear as main characters in the stories.

Younger women were often strong in a different way. In one novel, a very determined woman had been given a cattle ranch by a male relative and was competently running it when the hero came into her life. She and the hero teamed up against a wealthy rancher who was bent on overrunning her land with his large cattle herd, pushing her and the neighbors out. With the help of the lone rider hero, the threat was finally destroyed.

But not all women on the frontier could compete on an equal footing with males when it came to gun violence. In *Under the Sweetwater Rim,* two women, Mary (the hero's love interest) and Belle, were holed up in a cave with an army sergeant named Schwartz while Ten Brian had gone out to confront the outlaws. They heard distant gunfire and Mary wanted to go help him.

" 'There is nothing we can do,' Belle said. 'We must wait'.

'We could help him.'

'Ma'am,' Schwartz said gently, 'now he's got only himself to worry about, and maybe getting that payroll back. If you were over there he'd have to think about carin' for you, and that would most likely get himself killed. Believe me, ma'am, when it comes to guns a man had best have a mind for nothing but the other man and himself.' "

L'Amour, in *North to the Rails,* depicted a totally different type of woman. Sarah and her brother, Paul, came into the story late. They tried to murder Tom Chantry for his cattle herd and nearly succeeded. Kiowas later killed Paul. But Sarah, the greedy, murderous one of the pair, still tried to steal the $50,000 in gold the cattle were sold for at the railhead. L'Amour described her as completely amoral—a woman who would do anything to satisfy her lust for gold. Murder to her was like swatting a pesky fly. She teamed with other outlaws to help her, but all the time she was using her feminine wiles to pit the men against each other. After a big shootout, she managed to escape with all the gold by herself. With a map someone had drawn for her, she headed for Texas, leading a packhorse loaded with stolen gold. Unbeknownst to her, the map was not drawn to scale and Tascosa turned out to be hundreds of miles away, across the Staked Plains (the infamous *Llano Estacado*). She never reached Tascosa. The packhorse with the gold got away from her and was later picked up by her pursuers. But they never caught up with Sarah. Two cowboys, who briefly wondered how a woman had come to die of thirst miles from anywhere, found her bones thirteen years later.

The Spanish introduced the horse to the new world and within a few years, the whole way of life for the Indians changed. Horses became prized possessions and were a measure of an Indian's wealth to be bartered for a wife, or sold or traded for other goods.

CHAPTER 6

INDIANS

'Amour was careful to identify the particular tribes by name in areas where his stories took place. Yet, he rarely gave any detailed descriptions of their clothing, body paint, hair, weapons, saddles, customs, or any of the obvious things that would differentiate one tribe from another.

Once in a while an Indian would appear as a minor character, such as the friendly Cherokee, Ironhide, in *Under the Sweetwater Rim*.

Another minor character in *Kilrone* was the tall young woman, Mary Tall Singer, a Bannock Indian who was raised by whites. This mysterious girl stayed in the background through most of the novel, and several characters wondered whose side she would be on if the Bannocks, under Medicine Dog, attacked the fort. In the end, she came down on the side of the whites when she shot a Bannock warrior she knew, just as he was about to tomahawk one of the white defenders. (The idea for this novel could have been based on the Bannock War of 1878).

In the novel *North to the Rails,* Tom Chantry made a friend and ally of the English-speaking Pawnee, Sun Chief, who had formerly served under Frank North as an army scout against his ancient enemies the Sioux and Cheyenne.

One of the few Comanche leaders of whom we have several portraits by different photographers is Esitoya, translated as "Grey Leggings." In the early 1870s he led a band of Penateka Comanches and was also known for guiding Colonel Grierson to the site of Fort Sill and acting as a scout for the US troops on other occasions. When he died in 1878, his funeral was attended by the Fort Sill garrison, and he was buried in the post cemetery.

By the time of the great western migration in the mid- to late nineteenth century, some of the smaller tribes encountered by Lewis and Clark along the Missouri River had died out from diseases against which they had no resistance. During the post-Civil War period, the major tribes located in the Great Plains were the Sioux, Northern Cheyenne, Southern Cheyenne, Kiowa, Pawnee, and Comanche. Farther west in the Rockies lived the Ute, Arapaho, Bannock, Nez Perce, Blackfeet, and Crow. On the Pacific side of the mountains lived the Shoshone, Ute, Modoc, and Paiute. In the southwest were the Apache, Hopi, Navajo, Pueblo, Papago, Mojave, and Yuma. Numerous other smaller tribes were also scattered around and within these larger regions. All the western tribes were depicted as warlike opponents.

Even though his own great-grandfather (whom he never knew) had been killed and scalped by the Sioux, L'Amour seemed to be somewhat neutral on the subject of Indians. In his books, he depicted them as antagonists without attempting to get into their point of view or going into any detail about their habits, religion, or way of life.

Here was the narrator in the novel, *Kilrone,* from the point of view of a cavalry officer, "Captain Mellett had fought the Sioux and the Cheyenne, the Arapaho, Kiowa, and Comanche, the Nez Perce, and the Apache, and he knew what an Indian was like. The Indian he knew as a wily and dangerous warrior, a first-class fighting man who had his own set of rules and his own ideas of bravery."

L'Amour lumped them together, reluctantly praising them as fighters but wary of them as opponents. A bit later, Mellett was discussing Indians with another soldier and mentioned that the Mongol tribes, after fighting each other, had been united by Genghis Khan and, as a single force, conquered Europe. He was thankful the Indians had not put aside their tribal hatreds and done the same thing, or the whites would not have had a chance against them.

Above: Farther west in the Rockies lived the Ute, Arapaho, Bannock, Nez Perce, Blackfeet, and Crow. Pictured is Crow warrior Two Whistles wearing a medicine hawk headdress, war paint, a buckskin shirt, and shell necklaces. **Opposite top:** Pictured is arguably the most famous Native American of the Old West, Geronimo (on horseback with hat). The Apache medicine man (contrary to popular belief, he wasn't a chief, but he did lead battles) was wounded many times but always recovered, and as late as 1897, he was still boasting to those who would listen that no bullet could kill him. Indeed, foes and followers alike thought that Geronimo was endowed with supernatural powers. Eyewitnesses also declared him clairvoyant; according to them, he could interpret signs, explain the unknowable, and predict the future. **Opposite bottom:** Quanah Parker (seated, second from left) was the son of a Comanche warrior and a white woman who had been captured by the Indians. He became the last Comanche Chief and was a fierce warrior until the day in 1875 when he led his people to Fort Sill, Oklahoma, and took on a new, peaceful life. After giving up the warrior life and settling on the reservation, Quanah Parker became an advocate for his tribe and earned the respect and friendship of such notable figures as President Theodore Roosevelt.

In *The Lonely Men*, the narrator opined that the downfall of the various tribes was caused mainly when Indians became dependent on white men's goods, primarily tools, guns, and ammunition. L'Amour did not look upon those of his own race as cruel aggressors, beating up on the poor, primitive natives. He took the long view of history and saw each group of people who occupied the land as merely one link in a chain stretching back in time. Various tribes of Indian people had forced someone else off the land centuries before, and now people who were stronger and had a technologically superior culture, in turn, were forcing them out. Such changes, he believed, were the natural evolution of human societies in world history.

L'Amour's characters—especially those in the cavalry who had the job of trying to subdue the warlike tribes—realized that extermination of the buffalo herds was vital to the mission. Many tribes on the plains and the foothills of the Rockies depended for their very existence on the buffalo, which provided nearly all their food, shelter, clothing, and implements. Without the buffalo, these nomadic hunters would be helpless before the encroaching whites. L'Amour saw the buffalo being replaced by cattle herds, which would be replaced later by farmers growing crops to feed millions. He did not differentiate between the smaller prairies of the Mississippi Valley and the central and western high plains that had to depend on scarce rain or irrigation for abundant crops.

Opposite top: Attack of the Seventh Cavalry commanded by General Custer at the Cheyenne camp on the Washita River at dawn, November 27, 1868. L'Amour often mentioned the bravery and fighting skills of Native Americans in his novels.
Opposite bottom: Many tribes on the plains and the foothills of the Rockies depended for their very existence on the buffalo, which provided nearly all their food, shelter, clothing, and implements. Without the buffalo, these nomadic hunters would be helpless before the encroaching whites.

In his novel, *The Iron Marshal,* a character speaking to an immigrant said, " 'You mark my words, one day this prairie where only buffalo ranged will feed half the world. We have been killing the buffalo. Magnificent as they are, a man must decide what his values are, and you can grow no crops where buffalo range. There's no fence will stop them.' "

The nomadic Indians of the late 1800s L'Amour wrote about recognized no property lines between tribes—only a general understanding of what territory each group would use (often a shifting boundary decided by force). They had no concept of personal "land ownership." That idea came with encroaching whites. To most Indians, one might just as well claim to own a piece of the sky. The earth was there for all to occupy and use and would be there long after their children's children were gone. Some tribes did go to war over the exclusive right to certain hunting grounds or places they considered sacred. Long before any Europeans showed up, the nomadic hunting tribes raided each other to steal, kill, take prisoners, and display the bravery of their young warriors.

In *The Daybreakers,* an old frontiersman named Rountree had this to say: "Folks back east do a sight of talkin' about the noble red man . . . Folks talk about takin' land from the Injuns. No Injun ever *owned* land, no way. He hunted over the country and he was always fightin' other Injuns just for the right to hunt there." He went on to detail how Indians were taught as children: "There was none of this talk of mercy and kindness and suchlike we get from the time we're youngsters." Referring to Indians in general, he remarked, "Well, he's a mighty fine fighter, I give him that."

The Spanish introduced the horse to the new world. Invariably, Indians stole some, while others escaped into the wild and began to reproduce. Within a few years, the whole way of life of the Indians changed. Wild herds multiplied in the vast open spaces. Horses became prized possessions

Above left: Even though his own great-grandfather (whom he never knew) had been killed and scalped by the Sioux, L'Amour seemed to be somewhat neutral on the subject of Indians. In his books, he depicted them as antagonists without attempting to get into their point of view or going into any detail about their habits, religion, or way of life. This 1890 portrait is unique in that it isn't in a studio, and the Blackfoot warrior isn't dressed up in his finery. **Above right:** The Indians in L'Amour's novels and short stories were almost always antagonists. They provided a lurking presence of danger almost constantly. Even when they weren't actively stirring up trouble for the settlers, pioneers, or the army, they were out there, uncontained and ready to strike wherever and whenever they chose. Pictured is Cheyenne Little Bear in 1875. **Left:** Even though the various tribes of the Old West could have entirely different cultures and dress, L'Amour chose not to go into very many details of those aspects of Native American life. The Indians of the Pacific Northwest certainly had a very distinctive look as typified by Tlingit chief Ano-Tlosh in this 1906 photograph.

The nomadic Indians of the late 1800s that L'Amour wrote about recognized no property lines between tribes—only a general understanding of what territory each group would use (often a shifting boundary decided by force). They had no concept of personal "land ownership." That idea came with encroaching whites. To most Indians, one might just as well claim to own a piece of the sky.

and were a measure of an Indian's wealth to be bartered for a wife or sold or traded for other goods. The animals became one of the major prizes of raiding war parties. To the Plains Indians, especially, the coming of the horse must have seemed like a gift from the gods. The horse put wings to the plodding feet of the Indian. Suddenly, they had the equivalent of cars and trucks where before they were limited to the foot speed of their young men and the dogs that pulled their travois. Buffalo hunting could now be successful through sheer speed, and not just trickery and guile. According to statements from some US Army officers, the Plains Indians developed into some of the world's most skillful cavalry.

The Indians in L'Amour's novels and short stories were almost always antagonists. They provided a lurking presence of danger almost constantly. Even if they weren't actively stirring up trouble for the settlers, pioneers, or the Army, they were out there, uncontained and ready to strike wherever and whenever they chose. And, because of their mastery of the horse, they could strike and be gone, then strike again somewhere else. The horse made them mobile and much more dangerous than they would have been afoot, as was the case when mounted Spaniards terrified the Indians of Mexico in the sixteenth century. The Aztecs at first thought horse and armored rider were all one monstrous creature.

Right: A photograph from around the turn of the century portrays a domestic scene among Navajos near Old Fort Defiance in New Mexico. **Above:** This rare view of a Brule Indian village on the River Brule near Pine Ridge, South Dakota, gives one a feeling of what it might have been like to happen upon a Native American camp on the Great Plains. **Opposite top:** A captive white boy, Santiago McKinn, poses with a group of children in Geronimo's Camp in 1886, shortly before Geronimo's surrender to General George Crook on March 27, 1886. Chiricahua Apaches took McKinn from his home near Mimbres in the New Mexico Territory in 1885. The boy assimilated with the Apaches during his captivity—even learning their language—and cried when he was returned to his family. **Opposite bottom:** What's left of Big Foot's Miniconjou band (a subtribe of the Dakotas) in a tepee camp, probably on or near the Pine Ridge Reservation in South Dakota in 1891. Big Foot encouraged his people to adapt to life on the reservation by developing sustainable agriculture and building schools for Lakota children.

CHAPTER 7

READING SIGN

ouis L'Amour was fond of stating that he used actual places—springs, trails, mountains, and other natural features in his stories that could be identified if a reader wanted to go there and look. This was very often true. In addition to owning and using a collection of large-scale topographical maps, he did a lot of personal exploration of the country.

After the war when he'd settled in Los Angeles, was still single, and had no family responsibilities, he sometimes took breaks from his writing to travel back into the wild country of northern Arizona and immerse himself in the solitude of the settings he was using for his stories. Carrying a backpack, he would "hike some of the branch canyons that open into the Grand Canyon.... There were many trails that lead down to the river." He usually spent several days on these jaunts. "Not being much of a camp cook, I usually carried nuts, raisins, and a couple of small cans that could be opened easily," he wrote. "Several times I slept in Indian ruins, old cliff dwellings long abandoned by the Anasazi and their neighbors. There were ghosts around of course. Once a bear came along down the path past a ruin in which I was camped. He could not see me, but he caught my scent and

Opposite: L'Amour liked to write about real places and did lots of hiking and exploring in the Southwest, traveling from his home base in Los Angeles. This inviting scene is a creek along Andreas Canyon in the Agua Caliente Indian Reservation near Palm Springs, California, and would have been typical of some of the places L'Amour sought out.

Above: Bell Rock near Sedona, Arizona, would have been a train ride away for Louis L'Amour when he lived in Los Angeles during the prime of his writing career. He kept track of his travels with detailed notes and by utilizing his collection of large-scale topographical maps.

Top: During his solo explorations, L'Amour saw lots of wildlife in the silence of these wilderness areas—deer, soaring hawks, bobcats. "It was an easy, lazy time," he said. "I never had a set schedule to follow; no one was waiting for me or expected me." **Bottom:** In his autobiography L'Amour wrote, "Several times I slept in Indian ruins, old cliff dwellings long abandoned by the Anasazi and their neighbors. There were ghosts around of course." Pictured is the best-known cliff dwelling in the country at Mesa Verde National Park in Colorado.

Above: In the environment of the nineteenth-century West, the very survival of a lone traveler in a country swarming with hostiles, outlaws, and wild animals, depended on a man's ability to know the country and to read and interpret what he saw, as well as to blend into the background so as to make himself unseen by any possible enemy or pursuer. **Right:** Chromolithograph illustration of American frontiersman and US marshal Wild Bill Hickok (born James Butler Hickok, 1837–1876) as he fights a bear, in the mid to late nineteenth century. Although some of his exploits as reported at the time were quite fictionalized, his real skills as a gunfighter and gambler, along with his reputation as a lawman, provided the basis for his enduring fame.

sniffed around, hesitated and then went about his business. It was the right decision for both of us."

He saw other wildlife in the silence of these wilderness areas—deer, soaring hawks, bobcats. "It was an easy, lazy time," he went on. "I never had a set schedule to follow; no one was waiting for me or expected me. When I got tired of sleeping on the ground, I would head for the highway, often hitching a ride with an Indian in his pickup. Then I would take a bus or a train ride back to Los Angeles and hole up for another long stretch of writing."

Forty years later, he wrote in his autobiography, "People often ask me if I ride horseback. To tell you the truth, I have not been on a horse in years. Yet there is no reason why one should ride a horse to write about it, and I did my riding in the past. Now I ride to the sites I wish to explore in a four-wheel-drive vehicle and then get out and hike."

And he absorbed the details of what he saw. In his autobiography, *Education of a Wandering Man,* he stated, "Personally, I believe children should be taught to see, to observe, and to subject what they have seen to analysis, and this in the earliest grades." The heroes in his stories did observe and analyze and interpret what the natural signs were telling them. In the environment of the nineteenth-century West, the very survival of a lone traveler in a country swarming with hostiles, outlaws, and wild animals depended on a man's ability to know the country and to read and interpret what he saw, as well as to blend into the background so as to make himself unseen by any possible enemy or pursuer.

A typical fictional hero was a man experienced in the ways of the wilderness and of his hostile pursuers. He could elude Indian war parties by riding in streams and coming out on the opposite bank (a well-known dodge that even Tom Sawyer was familiar with). This hero knew that crossing sand dunes would leave no tracks that could be identified, that the age of tracks in snow could be judged by the slight melting of the sharp edges of the prints, and could closely estimate the amount of remaining daylight by the angle of the sun. "Skylining" on a mesa or hilltop was a sure way for an enemy to spot you, so a man always kept himself and his horse below the ridgeline to keep from showing a silhouette against the background of sky. He knew that wild horse bands followed a roughly circular route over a forty or fifty-mile area but always returned to their source of water. L'Amour's astute hero could feel a horse's hide in the dark and identify the brand. He knew the cream-colored flowers of the Cliff Rose, when crushed and boiled, were used by the Hopi to bathe wounds. Sometimes using field glasses as an aid to long-distance vision, L'Amour's heroes were able to distinguish a faint dust plume in the distance and identify it as being made by a wild horse herd, a single horseman, or a group of riders who might be on his trail. Even though they were similar, he could distinguish deer tracks from bighorn sheep tracks. One of his characters, an experienced Indian fighter, stated he could tell, by the smell of them, if Apaches had just left the reservation. How he could distinguish this, L'Amour did not explain. The character could tell if the Apaches had come off the desert after a long ride because the droppings of their horses showed fibers of desert plants they would eat only if nothing else was available. A L'Amour hero built small campfires either at dawn or dusk when the small amount of smoke would blend with an opaque sky and not be noticed from a distance, or he built small cooking fires under foliage where the smoke would be dissipated as it rose. If he was forced to camp upwind of his adversary, he made a dry camp with no fire at all. He often heard the call of a quail around sundown. He knew that buzzards always went for the eyes and kidneys first. He could find water in dry country by following animal tracks or a faintly defined animal trail leading downhill. On at least two occasions, a L'Amour protagonist found water by watching porcupines digging in the sand of a dry creek bed. He ran them off and continued digging to find water where the animals had smelled it. When trapped, he often escaped pursuit by finding and following a faint game trail, or the tracks of a cougar or mountain sheep over some precipitous rocky defile. He knew that cattle grazing along the Texas Gulf Coast liked the grass because it contained plenty of salt.

A man conversant with the desert was aware that cholla was known as the "jumping cactus" for good reason. Its clumps of needle-thin, translucent spines seemed to detach themselves from the plant, "jump out," and stick into anyone barely brushing them.

A L'Amour cowboy, familiar with livestock, knew how to chop a long, narrow hole in the ice of a frozen creek so several cattle could line up and drink at the same time as if at a trough. In addition, this cowhand would scatter dead leaves and brush on the ice to give the cattle better footing.

Finding himself high in the snowy Rockies or in the midst of a northern plains winter, a L'Amour protagonist knew that intense cold would stop bleeding quickly. He could build a fire of dead limbs in snow country, then hang a ground cloth behind it or place the fire near a cliff face as a reflector for warmth. He was adept at cutting and placing thick pine boughs to cushion his bedroll and make a soft, dry bed in the snow.

If an enemy was trailing him, he never stared into a campfire, knowing it would cause temporary night blindness; he slept away from the campfire and picketed his horse where he could not be

A typical fictional hero in a L'Amour novel was a man experienced in the ways of the wilderness and of his hostile pursuers. This photograph captures the essence of an old Ojibwe trapper.

Though it was the southwest part of the country that most often played host to L'Amour's novels, the northern Rocky Mountains were included in some settings as well. Pictured is a sedge marsh, in boreal Alberta, Canada.

easily spotted and stolen. He was always on guard against sudden attack.

A L'Amour man would not only be able to read sign and possess a vast knowledge of the natural world in which he traveled, but would also have an intuitive, animal-like ability to sense danger or the presence of other humans or animals, even when his physical senses detected nothing. One character, hardened to lone desert travel, was sitting his horse in total darkness alongside a head-high boulder and somehow sensed the presence of another human only a few yards away—a person he could neither see, hear, nor smell. Even though the man, himself, had no explanation of how it worked, perhaps science might say he was unconsciously picking up subliminal signals.

One example of reading sign and making a correct interpretation of its meaning was a L'Amour hero looking for the body of a dead bighorn sheep at night. He finally detected the faintest blur of white. After a few moments, he correctly identified it as the white belly hair of the bighorn carcass.

In one of his novels, a cavalry officer was questioning his civilian scout, a former Tennessean named Turpenning, about the sign he'd read while tracking some renegade white outlaws.

"Sign reads plain enough," Turpennng told him. "West and Dorsey rode together with a packhoss. Looks as if West had the payroll and was started back. Then Dorsey evidently shot him . . . leastways that's the way it reads." Knowing he was looking for two men, the scout had read the direction, number and depth of the hoof prints and also the blood he'd found.

Often when the cavalry was trailing a band of Indians, or outlaws wise in the ways of natives, the heavily-beaten trail of hooves diverged into two trails, then split again and yet again until there were so many individual trails they were impossible to follow. After the outlaws or hostile Indians had completely confused and frustrated their pursuers, they would meet up several miles later at some predetermined spot.

If a L'Amour character was primarily a desert man, he would be familiar with all kinds of plants—ocotillo, the century plant (agave), the spiny cholla, the upraised arms of the saguaro, Spanish bayonet (yucca) whose thorn and fibers

Above: Louis L'Amour was fond of stating that he used actual places—springs, trails, mountains, and other natural features in his stories that could be identified if a reader wanted to go there and look. Pictured is The Delicate Arch at sunset, in Arches National Park near Moab, Utah. **Left:** If a L'Amour character was primarily a desert man, he would be familiar with all kinds of plants, including the barrel cactus (pictured) whose pulpy inside, though distasteful, could be squeezed for a small drink, and prickly pear cactus, which produced edible fruit in season (jam is still made from it).

could provide a natural needle and thread for sewing, barrel cactus whose pulpy inside, though distasteful, could be squeezed for a small drink, and prickly pear cactus, which produced edible fruit in season (jam is still made from it). He would know that the mesquite bush produced beans which were edible when food was scarce, that the common creosote and mesquite bushes and dried manure were all good for building small campfires in the absence of wood. It was a bonus to know that creosote wood smoke imparted a good taste to beans. At a glance, he recognized ironwood, *palo verde,* and cat claw. L'Amour used the name Manzanita. This was a general term for a variety of low desert shrubs that function as groundcover for wide areas. They generally contained small, but very durable, branches. Chaparral cock, rabbits,

kangaroo rats, and wild *javelina* were among desert animals that could provide food in an emergency—*if* he could catch, kill, and cook them. A sidewinder would squirm down into the sand for protection from the sun, but if a man could somehow corner a diamondback rattler in the summer sun for only a few minutes, it would die. And rattlesnake meat was very tasty.

One of L'Amour's desert travelers said, "In much of the southwestern desert there's even a lot of green, although the *playas,* or dry lake beds, are dead white. Some of the desert plants hold back until there's a rain, then they leaf out suddenly and blossom quickly, to take advantage of that water. But much of the greenness of desert plants doesn't mean that rain has fallen, for many of the plants have stored water in their pulpy tissues

Above: A savvy man of the wilderness would know that a sidewinder will squirm down into the sand for protection from the sun, but if a man could somehow corner a diamondback rattler in the summer sun for only a few minutes, it would die. And rattlesnake meat was very tasty. **Right:** Chaparral cock, rabbits, kangaroo rats, and wild *javelina* (pictured) were among desert animals that could provide food in an emergency—*if* a man could catch, kill, and cook them.

to save against drought; others have developed hard-surfaced leaves that reflect sunlight and give off no moisture to the sun."

He went on to make the practical observation: "Plants and animals have learned to live with the desert, and so have the Apaches."

Knowing one's enemy was nearly as important as being able to read sign. A hardened desert traveler had to know the hostile Apache. An experienced desert man knew that Apache moccasins had harder leather soles than the moccasins of the Plains Indians because the rocks and spines of the desert were harder on the feet. A L'Amour hero of the Southwest stated he'd never known an Apache to eat fish; they preferred horse meat, and especially mule meat.

When under siege by stalking Apache warriors, it was vital to know they were immeasurably patient and might take hours to inch along, undetected, holding a small bush in front of them for camouflage and blending into the landscape. L'Amour often stated that Apaches would not fight at night because they believed, if killed, their souls would wander forever in the dark. At least that was the superstition the whites *thought* the Indians believed. Whenever possible, Apaches removed their dead after an attack. Thus, it was often impossible for whites to count enemy casualties.

The ability to read sign was often the difference between life and death.

Nat Bodine, the main character in the short story "Desert Death Song," was being pursued by a posse for a crime he did not commit. They finally cornered him in a jumble of rocks. Men intent on capturing or shooting him surrounded him on three sides. By sheer determination, he managed to climb down a near vertical cliff and escape into a waterless desert.

When the posse finally caught up two days later to tell him the real killer had been discovered and captured, they found Bodine alive and well with plenty of water. He told them he had seen a bee,

One of L'Amour's characters saved himself from dying of thirst by following the call of a certain kind of desert toad, which he knew lived by water.

then another, then several. Knowing bees had to have water, he tried to follow their erratic flight as best he could for a day and a half. After he finally lost track of them, he heard a noise that saved his life. It was a toad. As he related it, "That kind of toad never gets far from water. You only find them near some permanent seepage or spring. I was all in, down on my hands and knees when I heard him cheeping.

"It's a noise like a cricket, and I'd been hearing it some time before I remembered that a Yaqui had told me about these frogs. I hunted and found him so I knew there had to be water close."

In *The Lonely Men,* the first-person narrator telling the story said, "The desert is the enemy of the careless . . ." He went on to state that a man "travels slow to save himself, he keeps his eyes open to see those signs which indicate where water might be found. The flight of bees, or birds, the tracks of small animals, the kind of plants he sees—these things he must notice, for certain plants are indications of ground water, and some birds and animals never live far from water. Others drink little, or rarely, getting the moisture they need from the plants they eat or the animals they kill."

Above: A man in tune with the wilderness would be keen to the alarm signals sent out by animals such as ravens. The ability to read sign was often the difference between life and death, and many frontiersmen made it a priority to always learn from their experiences, no matter how minute. **Opposite:** For most of the year, the desert consists of fairly muted coloring. However, following the brief spring rainy season, incredible colors pop up for few short weeks.

Another instance of reading sign in nature to detect danger was given in the novel *Under the Sweetwater Rim*. Ten Brian, while fishing in a trout stream in the high mountains, had just pointed out to two young women the presence of a nearby bird called a "dipper," which actually walked on the bottom of the shallow stream to fish. "If you know the habits of birds and animals you can tell if anyone is around, just by the way they conduct themselves," he told them.

"But what about us? Doesn't our being here affect them at all?" one of them asked.

"Yes, but we've been quiet, no sudden moves…we're part of the picture," Brian answered her. "If you are in the forest and you remain quiet, birds and animals accept you. Oh, they'll keep an eye on you, but if you show no disposition to trouble them they will take you on your own terms. If anybody else comes up, off they go. And you are warned."

At night, the sudden cessation of chirping crickets was warning of a disturbing presence. In the daytime, a startled flock of quail, or grazing deer suddenly bounding away could deduce the same thing.

CHAPTER 8

FOOD AND TRANSPORTATION

In his novels, L'Amour did not overly emphasize food or what his characters were eating, except in a negative sense, when they were often hungry and thirsty, or due to some dire situation in the story, had not eaten for two or three days. He did mention now and then that someone was eating antelope steak or venison. When on the trail, a rider would often carry strips of jerky in his saddlebags as sustainable rations when he had nothing to cook and no time to cook it.

A description L'Amour did linger over now and then was the preparation and consuming of homemade doughnuts. Men who had been on the trail, or prospecting, or punching cows would flock to any man or woman who had doughnuts for sale. L'Amour's characters, without exception, loved doughnuts second only to homemade apple pies. After subsisting on mostly staples of bacon and beans and coffee, homemade doughnuts were a real luxury. Apparently, they were not difficult to make. They were known as bear sign (because they resembled bear scat). They were also referred to in *Hanging Woman Creek* as "sinkers" and "crullers."

One food item besides bear sign that was a staple in nearly all of L'Amour's writing was coffee. His characters seemed to be constantly brewing coffee, or drinking coffee, or lamenting the lack of

Opposite: One food item that was a staple in nearly all of L'Amour's writing was coffee. His characters seemed to be constantly brewing coffee, drinking coffee, or lamenting the lack of coffee or the opportunity to build a campfire to brew it. **Below:** L'Amour's characters, without exception, loved doughnuts second only to homemade apple pies. After subsisting on mostly staples of bacon and beans and coffee homemade doughnuts were a real luxury.

Right: In the Old West, chuckwagon food typically included easy-to-preserve items like beans and salted meats, coffee, and sourdough biscuits. Food would also be gathered en route. On cattle drives, it was common for the "cookie" that ran the wagon to be second in authority only to the "trailboss." The cookie would often act as cook, barber, dentist, and banker. **Below:** The invention of the chuckwagon is attributed to Charles Goodnight, a Texas rancher who introduced the concept in 1866. Goodnight modified the Studebaker wagon, a durable army-surplus wagon, to suit the needs of cowboys driving cattle from Texas to sell in New Mexico. He added a "chuck box" to the back of the wagon with drawers and shelves for storage space and a hinged lid to provide a flat cooking surface. A water barrel was also attached to the wagon, and canvas was hung underneath to carry firewood.

coffee or the opportunity to build a campfire to brew it. It was a recurring activity in nearly every book. Coffee was both their food and drink. They couldn't subsist on it but couldn't do without it. In nearly every situation where there was a slight pause in the action, the horses unsaddled, a fire kindled, the coffee pot was hauled out of the saddlebags, beans crushed and thrown into a pot of boiling water. It was brewed for breakfast, whether they had any food or not. It was brewed and drunk with supper around the campfire, or in the bunkhouse, or the ranchhouse, or under some sheltering overhang in the mountains. It was brewed and drunk even by the defenders of a fort that was being besieged by hundreds of Indians.

It was drunk without cream, and sugar was seldom available. There were no fancy coffees with whipped cream, cinnamon, and a variety of flavors and names as there are today. Coffee was indispensable for survival and was supposedly brewed so strong that it could float an iron horseshoe. Apparently L'Amour himself must have loved coffee since there is so much of this in his writing.

In his short story "Booty for a Badman," he did go into a bit more detail about an unusual type of food:

"The coffee was mostly ground bean and chicory, and all else I had was jerked venison and cold flour.

When the coffee was ready I filled my cup and passed it to her. 'Mrs. Mallory, this isn't what you have been used to, but it's all we've got.'

She tasted it, and if she hadn't been a lady, I think she would have spit, but she swallowed and then drank some more. 'It's hot,' she said and smiled at me, and I grinned back at her. Truth to tell, that was about all a body could say for it.

'You'd better try some of this jerked venison,' I said. 'If you hold it in your mouth awhile before you begin to chew, it tastes mighty wholesome. All else I've got is cold flour.'

'What?'

'Cold flour—it's a borrowed thing, from the Indians. Only what I have here is white-man style. It's parched corn ground up and mixed with a mite of sugar and cinnamon. You can mix it with water and drink it, and a man can go for miles on it. Mighty nourishing too. Pa was in Montana one time and traveled two weeks on a couple of dry quarts of it.' "

Occasionally he did mention a brand name—Arbuckles—which became known as the "Coffee that Won the West." It was famous in its day.

TRANSPORTATION

Being a writer of historic westerns, L'Amour naturally depicted his characters using horses, and sometimes mules, for personal transportation. Often mules were used for pack animals and sometimes horses as well. Smaller burros served as pack animals and were a favorite of prospectors. Sometimes lone prospectors treated these burros like pets and named them. One prospector had a burro he'd named Buster. But mostly, L'Amour's characters did not name their horses, unless he had a string of two or three, as some cowboys did. For example, narrator Tye Sackett in *The Daybreakers* had a string of horses he used on a cattle

Today many restored chuckwagons are used in cookoff competitions, racing, and in this particular scene, for tourists wanting to experience an Old West dude ranch experience at Trail Dust Town in Tucson, Arizona.

Top: Horses, mules, and donkeys were all utilized as a pulling force for wagons. Smaller burros were a favorite of prospectors, and sometimes lone prospectors treated these burros like pets and named them. **Above:** When it came to horses, L'Amour tended to give a visual image and avoided using the generic name "horse" all the time, sometimes identifying them by a visual description, such as a "long-legged zebra dun," or a "bay," a "black," a "buckskin," or "blue roan." He also called some by breed, such as a "Morgan," "Appaloosa," or even sometimes a "Mustang" (a mixed wild breed). **Right:** A mule train ascends the South Kaibab Trail at the Grand Canyon South Rim in Grand Canyon National Park, Arizona. The Grand Canyon is among the state's biggest tourist destinations and was a favorite of L'Amour's during his days of exploration.

Left: Pioneers who couldn't afford the big Conestoga wagons made sure they had the best farm wagon they could find, or reinforced a lighter wagon and affixed wooden bows covered by white, sun-reflecting canvas. These wagons were their traveling homes for months as the draft animals hauled wagons, people, and possessions more than fifteen hundred miles across the plains, rivers, and mountains to California or Oregon. **Below:** Big, boat-shaped Conestoga wagons pulled by ox teams were the best way to cross the country for pioneers who could afford one. These huge wagons could carry several tons of goods and people and were sealed watertight and curved up at each end so they could float across rivers like a clumsy boat.

drive and named them Dapple, Sate (Satan), and Buck (for buckskin). The author, however, to give a visual image and to keep from using the generic name "horse" all the time, sometimes identified them by a visual description such as a "long-legged zebra dun," or a "bay," a "black," or a "buckskin" or "blue roan." He also called some by breed, such as a "Morgan," "Appaloosa," or even sometimes a "Mustang" (a mixed wild breed).

Those westering pioneers who could afford it traveled in immigrant trains in the big, boat-shaped Conestoga wagons pulled by ox teams. These huge wagons could carry several tons of goods and people and were sealed watertight and curved up at each end so they could float across rivers like a clumsy boat. They were expensive, so it was not uncommon for families to band together to travel. Many pioneers of lesser means just made sure they had the best farm wagon they could find, or reinforced a lighter wagon and affixed wooden bows covered by white, sun-reflecting canvas. These wagons were their traveling homes for months as the draft animals hauled wagons, people, and possessions more than fifteen hundred miles across the plains, rivers, and mountains to California or Oregon. In very dry country, the wooden spokes in the wheels would shrink, sometimes causing the wheel to fall apart. If a stream was handy, or a water barrel could be spared for the purpose, the spokes were soaked overnight, allowing the wood to swell so they would again fit the rims.

Another common conveyance used by the military to haul all kinds of goods and people was the army ambulance, a sturdy Dougherty wagon. These L'Amour didn't bother to describe, but they were solidly built enclosed wagons with fairly tall, iron-rimmed wheels and pulled by teams of horses or mules. Even though ambulances were often used for general hauling or carrying passengers, their name indicated they were originally intended to transport the wounded or injured. Yet they were unsprung vehicles that must have made for a very jarring ride for anyone in pain.

Below left: This Wells Fargo stagecoach, which currently resides in the Wells Fargo Center in downtown Los Angeles, is a pristine example of the popular Concord wagon, which was manufactured in Massachusetts. It was a top-of-the-line coach and stood about eight feet high and weighed over a ton, costing between $1,200 and $1,500. **Below right:** Travelling through mountain passes in the nineteenth century meant navigating on treacherous, meandering trails that could very well have looked like this one. This is a modern view of a trail in Zion National Park in Utah.

Mark Twain, in his book *Roughing It,* was one well-known writer who gave an accurate, often hilarious, account of his stagecoach trip from St. Joseph, Missouri, to Virginia City, Nevada, in 1861. Twain and his brother traveled more than two weeks on a stagecoach across the Great Plains and the Rocky Mountains, visiting the Mormon community in Salt Lake City. His experiences in Angels Camp, California, in Calaveras County, provided material for "The Celebrated Jumping Frog of Calaveras County."

At the other extreme from the unsprung army ambulance was the regal Abbott Downing coach, also known as the Concord stagecoach from the town where it was manufactured—Concord, New Hampshire. The top-of-the-line coach stood about eight feet high and weighed over a ton and cost between $1,200 and $1,500. It had seats for nine passengers inside—three on each side, facing each other—with a low padded bench between them where another three could be seated. Besides the driver and guard, an unknown number of others could ride up top, clinging to the handrails or to the luggage boot in back. Photographs have shown as many as twenty-one passengers packed into and onto one of these coaches. The Concord was a marvel of design. They were usually painted in a bright color—often red—with contrasting yellow wheel rims and spokes, and some outdoor scene emblazoned on their sides. The name of the stage line was lettered near the top on each side, such as BUTTERFIELD LINE, or THE OVERLAND EXPRESS, or WELLS FARGO CO.

From his voluminous reading of diaries and journals of early pioneer travelers, L'Amour was well aware that many of them recorded details of grueling long-distance trips in stagecoaches. Concords were designed to be as comfortable as rough roads would allow, but a trip that lasted weeks could still be exhausting. Mark Twain, in his book *Roughing It,* was one well-known writer who gave an accurate, often hilarious, account of his stagecoach trip from St. Joseph, Missouri, to Virginia City, Nevada, in 1861.

The Concord coach was actually suspended on two fore-and-aft thoroughbraces—several thicknesses of doubled leather straps that were fastened to the front and rear axles. It cradled the passengers and luggage, protecting the riders inside and on top from the jolts and jarring ruts and holes as it pitched and rolled like a sailing vessel in high seas. Roll-down leather curtains on the windows were helpful in keeping out dust, rain, snow, or sun. It had tall rear wheels and somewhat shorter front ones (to aid in turning) but could ford streams that weren't too deep. These coaches were hauled by either four- or six-horse hitches, or sometimes mules. Except for stops at stage stations to change teams every fifteen or twenty miles, and maybe allow the passengers time for a bite to eat, and periodically to change drivers, these coaches ran day and night. Long distance passengers had to deal with fatigue, continuous bouncing, dust, heat, cold, rain, snow, sometimes breakdowns or Indians. Now and then passengers had to get out

Above: Virtually all trails originated in Independence, Missouri, a gateway to the American West. Perhaps the most famous wagon train trail was the Oregon Trail, which had a span of over 2,000 miles. Other paths included the Santa Fe Trail, the Chisholm Trail, the California Trail (which split southwestward from the Oregon Trail), the Mormon Trail, and the Old Spanish Trail. **Right:** The typical ore wagon was built of solid oak, had a bed sixteen feet long and six feet deep. The iron bands circling the wide wheel rims were an inch thick. Empty, one of these weighed 7,800 pounds!

and walk to lighten the load for a team pulling up some steep grade. But the big Concords were state-of-the-art public transportation in wild country in their day, until the railroads came along.

The Abbott Downing company made several sizes of these Concords and even made a smaller, lighter coach of a different design called the celerity coach (meaning "rapid"). They were designed for shorter hauls, weighed less than half what a big Concord weighed due to having canvas roofs and sides, and required less horsepower.

2347. Tallyho Coaching. Sioux City party Coaching at the Great Hot Springs of Dakota.
Photo and copyright by Grabill, 1889.

This 1889 party out of Sioux City heading to the Great Hot Springs of Dakota is taking place for an afternoon of sightseeing, rather than a long-distance commute. One would hope that the trail that day was smooth with no sharp inclines, as a fall from the top of this carriage appears to be quite a distance to the ground!

The ugly stepsister of the elegant Concord and the swifter celerity was something called the "mud wagon." This was exactly what the name implied—an open-sided wagon with a canvas top and side curtains and a lower center of gravity. Their wheels were not as tall and had a broader stance for stability. The wheel rims were wider so they wouldn't sink into mud or sand as easily. The vehicle required only a span of mules or horses for locomotion. Mud wagons were the 4-wheel drive utility vehicles of their day. Designed for rough work, they could go where others bogged down, slid off the road, or tipped over. Lower, wider, and solidly built, the mud wagon was a lighter passenger vehicle that could be pulled by fewer animals and could negotiate muddy roads, deep sand, snow and could go places the larger Concord could

not. It was not designed for comfort, but was generally used for shorter trips. In his books, L'Amour mentioned both the overland Concords as well as the smaller types of wagons.

In the days before gasoline or diesel engines, dozens of types of horse-drawn vehicles were in use—from light buggies and buckboards to the giant ore wagons whose wheels were seven feet tall. One of these is still on display in the streets of Tombstone, Arizona, and a typical three-wagon train is exhibited at Furnace Creek, Death Valley. The typical ore wagon was built of solid oak, had a bed sixteen feet long and six feet deep. The iron bands circling the wide wheel rims were an inch thick. Empty, one of these weighed 7,800 pounds!

L'Amour's characters in novels such as *The Comstock Lode* would have been familiar with

Top: Many a plot in western tales featured a "railroad is coming through town" twist. It was no exaggeration that the introduction of trains would drastically transform the town, the local Indian tribes, and the entire concept of getting goods and people in and out of the West. **Bottom:** A vintage photographer attempts to capture in one shot the incredible revolution in transportation that the mid-1800s heralded. With horses being first domesticated around 3,000 BC, having their dominance in transportation tumble in just a few decades became a major milestone in human history.

Above left: A Civil War–era *cartes de visite* (small albumen print) photo of a pioneer Iowa family of five is typical of the formal dress of the day. If the manner of dress of a character were unusual, L'Amour would go into more detail. **Above right:** A tin-type photograph of a married couple from late 1800s portrays a more gothic style of dress than in the earlier times.

these gigantic ore wagons. A well-known example of ore wagons used in early western mining could be seen in *Death Valley Days,* the popular TV program from the 1950s to 1960s. A company founded in 1877 that sold "20 Mule Team Borax" as a laundry detergent sponsored this long-running television series. Borax (sodium tetraborate, a naturally occurring substance produced by the repeated evaporation of seasonal lakes) was mined in the desert around Death Valley. In the early days, borax was transported from the mines by wagon train across the Mojave Desert to the closest railroad 165 miles away. A loaded train weighed just over 73,000 pounds and averaged about seventeen miles per day. These trains

operated from 1883 to 1889, when a railroad spur was built closer to the mines.

The trains themselves were an awesome sight, stretching nearly a hundred yards in length. The TV show opened with a shot of two huge ore wagons and a trailing water wagon pulled by a long hitch of twenty mules. The 20 Mule Team Borax brand became famous. The team and wagons were even exhibited at the 1904 St. Louis World's Fair and later caused amazement among spectators at a parade in New York City. In actuality, the team consisted of eighteen mules and two horses (who were the wheelers). Two men, a teamster and a swamper, operated the train. The teamster usually rode the left wheeler and controlled the eighteen

Despite the fact that these cowboys are in a photo studio, they appear to be wearing their own attire, even if it might be their "special, goin' to the barn dance duds." L'Amour commonly mentioned only those items of clothing that would allow the reader to form a mental image of the character.

mules in front of him with a long blacksnake whip. Sometimes, if he needed to operate the brake on a steep descent, he rode the seat on the trailer (the first wagon). The swamper assisted as needed but usually rode near the rear.

L'Amour commonly mentioned only those items of clothing that would allow the reader to form a mental image of the character. A cowboy or horseman might be wearing leather chaps—or, if he wanted to get specific, batwing-style chaps or those made of sheepskin. A hat could have a Montana peak or be flat crowned and straight brimmed. Vests were standard attire, mostly for use of their pockets. If men weren't wearing boots, L'Amour would usually mention their footgear, such as moccasins, and why they were wearing such an item of Indian apparel. Women he usually

described as being in a plain frock or a frilly gown, or if she were riding astride, she might be dressed in a pair of jeans or whipcord pants, a checkered blouse, and a hat.

If the manner of dress was unusual, L'Amour went into more detail, as in *The Daybreakers* when the narrator was describing Mexican freighters: "Their jackets were short, only to the waist, and their pants flared out at the bottom, and fitted like a glove along the thighs. Their spurs had rowels like mill wheels on them, and they all had spanking-new rifles and pistols. They wore colored silk sashes like some of those Texas cowhands wore, and they were all slicked out like some kind of a show."

When a rider mounted a California saddle, for example, and the reader knew what that was and

Above left: This hand-colored engraving of a Frederic Remington illustration portrays a Mexican *vaquero* (cowboy) from the late 1800s. **Above right:** Even though L'Amour had a lot of experience at sea, relatively few of his western stories took place on the ocean. A couple of his novels began there, such as *Crossfire Trail* that opened on a sailing vessel coming down the California coast. And *Matagorda* started with a scene of the characters arriving on the Texas Gulf Coast.

could picture it, then the realism of the story was enhanced. If the reader had no idea what kind of saddle that was, that lack did not detract from the story.

Even though L'Amour had a lot of experience at sea, relatively few of his western stories took place on the ocean. A couple of his novels began there, such as *Crossfire Trail* that opened on a sailing vessel coming down the California coast. And *Matagorda* started with a scene of the characters arriving on the Texas Gulf Coast.

Riverboats were another subject that was lightly dealt with. *Rivers West* did feature some rivers in Louisiana, but in a much earlier time period of the 1820s. *Ride the River,* a Sackett novel, was set in the East, a good portion of it in Philadelphia.

Much of the West was arid or mountainous country, but the Missouri River was navigable from St. Louis all the way to the mining camps of Montana. And there was the mighty Columbia flowing from the Rockies to the Pacific. For many years, even the Colorado River was alive with steamboat traffic, hauling passengers and freight from the Gulf of California to Yuma and all the way to the head of navigation in present-day northern Arizona. Even San Francisco Bay is rich with history. But, for reasons known only to him, L'Amour chose not to use these waterways as settings for his stories.

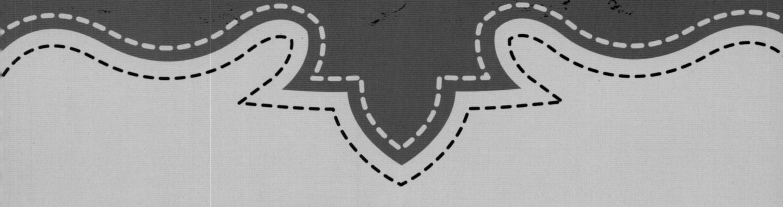

ARBUCKLES—THE COFFEE THAT WON THE WEST

Following the Revolutionary War, many Americans, perhaps to rid themselves of all things British, abandoned tea drinking and took up drinking coffee, a native product of the New World. But for more than three-quarters of a century, coffee drinkers had to buy their beans green and attempt to roast them before grinding and brewing their preferred drink.

It was necessary to sell the beans green because, after being roasted, they started losing their flavor and aroma within a couple of weeks through a chemical process involving oxidation. Thus, it was left up to the restaurant owner, or the individual consumer, to roast his own beans and then grind them for use. Roasting coffee beans evenly was a difficult process in a pan on a stove or over an open campfire. A few burned beans ruined the flavor.

But all this changed around 1865. Two brothers, John and Charles Arbuckle, partners in a grocery business in Pittsburgh, Pennsylvania, figured out a way to preserve the flavor and freshness of the coffee after it was roasted by sealing the porous surface of the beans with a glaze of eggs and sugar. They patented this process. Their coffee, marketed as Arbuckles Ariosa Coffee in one-pound sacks, quickly became the first commercially successful pre-roasted coffee on the market, and business boomed. Because the quality of flavor and aroma were consistent, and the preparation process simplified, it caught on as the drink of choice nationwide, and especially in the post–Civil War West on cattle drives, around campfires, in boomtowns, frontier settlements and ranches, and in restaurants along the newly built railroad lines.

The Arbuckle brothers sold their product in sacks with yellow labels and red lettering. As a marketing ploy, they inserted a peppermint stick into each one-pound package, along with a coupon redeemable for a variety of prizes such as razors and handkerchiefs. A 100-package wooden crate of their coffee was branded with the name ARBUCKLES COFFEE in large letters. There was no mistaking it for anything else.

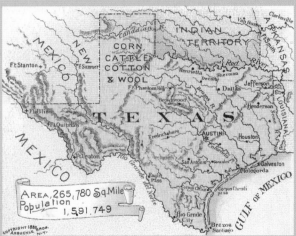

Top: Arbuckles Ariosa Coffee caught on as the drink of choice nationwide, and especially in the post–Civil War West on cattle drives, around campfires, in boomtowns, frontier settlements and ranches, and in restaurants along the newly-built railroad lines. **Bottom:** Arbuckles aggressively marketed their coffee, and one campaign that apparently was quite popular was the colorful series of maps and postcards the company produced. Note in this 1889 postcard rendition of Texas that the area we now know as Oklahoma is referred to as "Indian Territory"; it would not become a state until 1907.

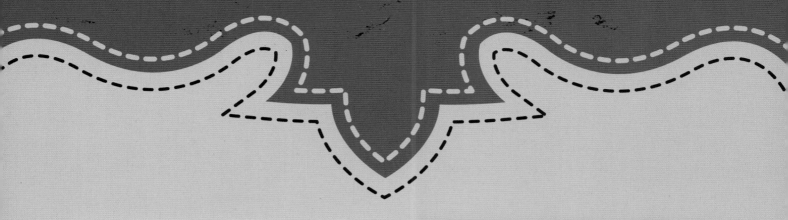

Western wear, music, and campfires are not only deeply ingrained in American popular culture, but also are well-known throughout the world as well, much of it having to do with literature such as L'Amour's. This photo postcard appears to be from around the mid-1950s.

Arbuckles became not only a brand name, but also a generic name for coffee, similar to the way Coke years later became a generic name for any cola drink.

Arbuckles could be toted anywhere and kept for long periods of time until someone decided to crush the beans and boil up a pot to drink. Along with flour, beans, and bacon, it became a staple of the frontier, a brand name on a par with Stetson and Colt.

Descendants of the Arbuckle brothers broke up the company in the early twentieth century, retaining only a special holiday blend called Yuban, a brand later sold to a large corporation.

The company was resurrected under the Arbuckles name several years ago and is once again going strong out of Tucson, Arizona.

Chapter 9

Writing Style and Lingo

Sometimes L'Amour wrote in the first person to tell his story through the main character. If the character happened to be an uneducated backwoodsman, he related the story in his own dialect as if telling the story aloud.

But, more often than not, L'Amour used the omniscient point of view. This style of writing allowed him to be in the minds of every character in the scene from moment to moment, switching points of view at will from sentence to sentence or paragraph to paragraph. It enabled the reader to continuously follow what each person was thinking and feeling as conversation proceeded and external events were taking place. Other western writers more often switched points of view at a scene break or at the beginning of a new chapter.

L'Amour wrote several novels featuring men who were members of a fictional extended family called the Sacketts who came from the Appalachian Mountains in east Tennessee. The men of this clan mostly lacked formal education and had different personalities, but they were all tough-minded, loyal to their values, and big, rawboned, fearless men. They were good with their fists but shy in polite society. The brothers, cousins, and uncles who migrated west from their isolated homes retained their unique mountain dialect. One of the regional quirks of speech was their frequent use of the word "taken" in place of the simple past tense, "took." For example, in one of the novels, L'Amour had William Tell Sackett say, "Reaching over, I taken up my rifle and jacked a shell into the chamber." This use of the past participle of the verb "take" can still be heard occasionally today from those who grew up in the Appalachian region of east Tennessee. Another example: "Billy Higgins and me, we taken out a-running, heading for the rocks where we could make a fight of it." The Sacketts were often depicted as being illiterate, but they had a survival instinct from their hard upbringing. Another expression L'Amour put in the mouths of these

Above left: In 1979, a two-part TV adaptation was made of L'Amour's third novel in the Sackett series. *The Sacketts* starred Glenn Ford (standing) as one of the lead cowboys in a cattle drive, with Tom Sellick (foreground) and Jeff Osterhage as two of the three Sackett brothers (Sam Elliott played the third). Viewers could also spot Ben Johnson, Slim Pickens, Jack Elam, and even Louis L'Amour making a cameo. **Above right:** One wonders how people of the Old West would interpret a sight such as this—220-million-year-old giant fossil conifer logs—during their travels. These logs were photographed littering a canyon in the Petrified Forest National Park in Arizona and probably haven't moved much more than a few inches since the 1880s.

characters was this: "My pappy always told me to fight shy of women (or, whatever subject he was discussing)." And two more, "... the Tinker knew things a body could scarcely keen, and held a canny knowledge of uncanny things" and "It ired me that he should think so..." These and other such expressions may be remnants of an earlier form of English, since language and culture of people isolated from mainstream society for generations were often slower to change.

An archaic expression one of the Sacketts used was not necessarily of mountain origin: "It was a caution what folks would do to lay hands on a few steers." Another idiom not of mountain origin was, "You boys on your uppers?" This was the local lawman talking to two hobos. The expression literally meant, "Have you been walking so long that you've worn the bottoms off your shoes until you're walking on the leather uppers?" In other words, he was asking if they were flat broke and down on their luck.

In the novel *Kilrone,* Hank Laban was a tough, experienced frontiersman scouting for a troop of cavalry. The old scout knew the glory-seeking major was leading his men into a trap, but the officer ignored Laban's advice. Laban had read the whole situation correctly, and privately decided to ride out fast when trouble came. The narrator

Above: How can one begin to describe with words alone a sight like this? These rock formations at Sunset Point in Bryce Canyon National Park (Utah) are known as the "Hoodoos." They were formed by frost weathering and stream erosion of the river and lakebed sedimentary rocks. **Right:** Referring to the harsh, unsettled West, L'Amour repeated in several different novels some form of the following expression: "Folks say this country is hell on horses and women."

described him thus: "Laban was an old coon from the high-up creeks, and he knew the signs."

L'Amour used the word "cove," meaning a flat, open piece of ground indented into the side of a hill or mountain. Such an actual place is the well-known Cades Cove in the Great Smoky Mountain National Park. Traditionally, this term is used only in its nautical sense to describe a small inlet or harbor.

Referring to the harsh, unsettled West, L'Amour repeated in several different novels some form of the following expression: "Folks say this country is hell on horses and women."

The caption under this 1904 stereo card reads, "Indian Braves, splendid with savage finery, riding their ponies down the Pike—World's Fair, St. Louis, U.S.A."

A plural of the word "hoof" always appears as "hoofs" in his novels, instead of the older, more common "hooves." English is constantly evolving, and this was possibly what his publisher adopted as their preferred usage.

L'Amour rarely used clichés in his narratives but sometimes allowed his characters to fall into them when speaking. For example, "Let's get down to brass tacks." Or, "That damn Mick would charge hell with a bucket o'water."

Although some writers still use the two words "further" and "farther" interchangeably, the former means "degree" and the latter refers to distance. L'Amour occasionally used "further" when talking about distance.

Many times in his novels, L'Amour repeated the statement that Apache warriors generally wouldn't fight in the dark because they believed the soul of a man killed at night wandered forever in darkness. This remark was always uttered by a character or the unseen narrator as a general belief—not as a statement of absolute fact.

Homemade doughnuts were referred to by nicknames such as "bear sign," "sinkers," and "crullers."

L'Amour, like other writers, often used the device of jumping into a story in the first sentence or paragraph. He had a lot of practice at this technique when he wrote short stories for the pulp magazines. He could figuratively grab the reader by the shirtfront, yank him up, and yell: "Listen to this! I've got a story to tell you."

As he put it, "I think of myself in the oral tradition—as a troubadour, a village tale-teller, the man in the shadows of the campfire. That's the

Opposite: L'Amour, like other writers, often used the device of jumping into a story in the first sentence or paragraph. He had a lot of practice at this technique when he wrote short stories for the pulp magazines. He could figuratively grab the reader by the shirtfront, yank him up, and yell: "Listen to this! I've got a story to tell you." **Opposite inset:** L'Amour's short story "The Gift of Cochise" was sold and made into the movie *Hondo,* starring John Wayne. Louis then wrote a novelization of the somewhat changed screenplay. Note the Duke's hearty endorsement at the bottom of the cover.

"Can't you hurry this up a bit? I hear they eat dinner in Hades at twelve sharp and I don't aim to be late," said Black Jack Ketchum, just before he was hanged at Clayton, New Mexico, on April 26, 1901. Some say, perhaps, that ghosts of the Old West still inhabit the remains of towns where people lived and died over 150 years ago.

way I'd like to be remembered—as a storyteller. A good storyteller."

He continued the practice of fast starts in his later short stories and many of his novels—an effective device for capturing the attention of readers. His short story "The Gift of Cochise" was sold and made into the movie *Hondo,* starring John Wayne. L'Amour then wrote a novelization of the somewhat changed screenplay. The short story began like this:

"Tense, and white to the lips, Angie Lowe stood in the door of her cabin with a double barreled shotgun in her hands. Beside the door was a Winchester '73, and on a table inside the house were two Walker Colts.

"Facing the cabin were twelve Apaches on ragged calico ponies, and one of the Indians had lifted his hand, palm outward. The Apache sitting the white-splashed bay pony was Cochise."

A reader would have to be rudely interrupted to put down a story beginning with such a tense life-or-death situation.

Above: L'Amour plucked a scene in *The Iron Marshal* directly from one of many similar incidents of his own past. As a young man, he'd ridden freights across the West, and had been caught by railroad "bulls" and dumped off in cold, dark, isolated places.

Right: Wild Bill Hickok (seated) was involved in several notable shootouts. He was shot from behind and killed while playing poker in 1876 at a saloon in Deadwood, Dakota Territory (now South Dakota) by an unsuccessful gambler, Jack McCall. The card hand he held at the time of his death (aces and eights) has come to be known as the "Dead Man's Hand." He is pictured with his associate Eugene Overton, who appeared in the Buffalo Bill Shows with Hickok in the "Scouts of the Trails" act.

The short story "Trap of Gold" opened with these lines:

"Wetherton had been three months out of Horsehead before he found his first color. At first, it was a few scattered grains taken from the base of an alluvial fan where millions of tons of sand and silt had washed down from a chain of rugged peaks; yet the gold was ragged under the magnifying glass." The reader would almost be compelled to read on and find out what was going to happen. Incidentally, this story was later expanded into the novel *Taggart*, which began this way: "Adam Stark was three months out of Tucson when he found his first color. It appeared as a few scattered flakes of gold dry-panned from the base of an alluvial fan, but the gold was rough under the magnifying glass."

Never one to waste a good premise or interesting characters with just one telling, L'Amour expanded several short stories into novels. "War Party" became the novel *Bendigo Shafter*. "Dutchman's Flat" later became the novel *The Key-Lock Man*.

L'Amour, himself, explained it like this:

"Almost forty years ago, when my fiction was being published exclusively in 'pulp' western magazines, I wrote several novel-length stories which my editors called 'magazine novels.' In creating them I became so involved with my characters that their lives were still as much a part of me as I was of them long after the issues in which they appeared became collector's items. Pleased as I was about how I brought the characters and their adventures to life in the pages of the magazines, I still wanted the reader to know more about my people and why they did what they did. So, over the years, I revised and expanded these magazine works into fuller-length novels that I published in paperback under other titles."

Expanding short stories into novels has been a common practice for many writers. Hemingway, for example, turned one of his short stories into the famous short novel *The Old Man and the Sea*.

L'Amour's novel *The Man from the Broken Hills* began like this:

"I caught the drift of woodsmoke where the wind walked through the grass.

"A welcome sign in wild country...or the beginning of trouble."

His novel *The Iron Marshal* opened with the lines:

"A brutal kick in the ribs jolted him from a sound sleep and he lunged to his feet. The kicker, obviously a railroad detective, stepped back and drew a gun.

"'Don't try it,' he advised. 'Just get off.'"

These were only a few examples of the way L'Amour began, *in medias res*—in the middle of things—an effective standard device of writers for ages.

L'Amour plucked this latter scene directly from one of many similar incidents in his past. As a young man, he'd ridden freights across the West, and had been caught by railroad "bulls" and dumped off in cold, dark, isolated places.

Now and then, L'Amour created a character who was well educated and spoke perfect English. But when this man wanted to blend into a rough background of working men in the West, he often let his good grammar and annunciation slide into the vernacular of whatever group he was mingling with. This was the case with French Williams, a mysterious man in *North to the Rails*.

Another example of this was a man who turned out to be from Ireland, but was careful to change his idiomatic expressions and his dialect when he was among cowboys and ranch hands.

Opposite: L'Amour and his editors at Bantam didn't necessarily catch every inconsistency in the texts. In *Last Stand At Papago Wells*, the hero was forced into a knife fight with an Apache on a moonless night, and there was this passage: "He came in low, the knife gleaming bright in the starlight..." Without any moonlight at all, stars by themselves would not give enough light to reflect a bright gleam from a knife blade.

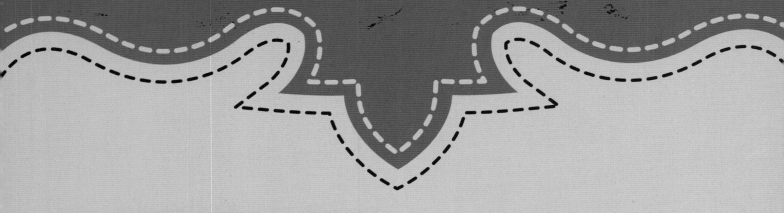

SLIP UPS AND MISCUES

Louis L'Amour wrote a lot of novels and he wrote them quickly. In order to keep his name and his work constantly before the reading public, his publisher, Bantam Books, urged him to write three books a year. Working steadily and tirelessly, he did this for thirty years. By his own admission, he didn't revise or rewrite, and he didn't always know where the story was going once he started. He relied on his intuition and writing skill and ideas coming to him as he wrote to arrive at a successful conclusion to a story. When he finished, he went on to the next book.

This method worked well, but it invariably led to discrepancies in details, which editors at Bantam Books didn't always catch or correct.

For example, in *The Quick and the Dead,* the main character felt a stab of agony in his side after being shot once.

Kilrone, hero of the novel by the same name, was trying to escape from a cavalry fort that was being attacked by hundreds of Bannock Indians. Pictured are a group of Bannocks, whose traditional lands include southeastern Oregon, southeastern Idaho, western Wyoming, and southwestern Montana.

Whiskey had a number of colorful names during the days of the Old West, including bottled courage, bug juice, coffin varnish, dynamite, fire water, gut warmer, joy juice, neck oil, nose paint, redeye, scamper juice, snake pizen, tarantula juice, tonsil varnish, tornado juice, and wild mare's milk.

Two chapters later, the reader discovered the bullet went through his thigh, not his body.

In *The Key-Lock Man* was the following passage (italics are mine): "It was early morning and *a slow smoke lifted from the chimney of the trading post*." A few sentences later, "Inside it was shadowed and cool. The adobe walls kept the coolness in and the heat of the sun out." In the same scene, L'Amour, the narrator, went on, "In a chair beside the *unused stove*, sat a stocky, muscular man, feet propped up." The unused stove was smoking?

In *Last Stand at Papago Wells*, the hero was forced into a knife fight with an Apache on a moonless night, and there was this passage: "He came in low, the knife gleaming bright in the starlight..." Without any moonlight at all, stars by themselves would not give enough light to reflect a bright gleam from a knife blade.

In *The Lonely Men*, an Indian gave William Tell Sackett a "Navy .44." This was very likely a simple slip-up. L'Amour knew as well as any other western author that a Colt revolver designated as a "Navy" was, by definition, a .36 caliber just as a single-action army revolver was, by definition, a .44 caliber.

In many of his novels where the story took place in the heat of the summer desert, L'Amour described his characters as sweating profusely. Sweat either ran down their faces and stung their eyes, or their gun hands were sweating from heat and nervousness, or they were wiping perspiration

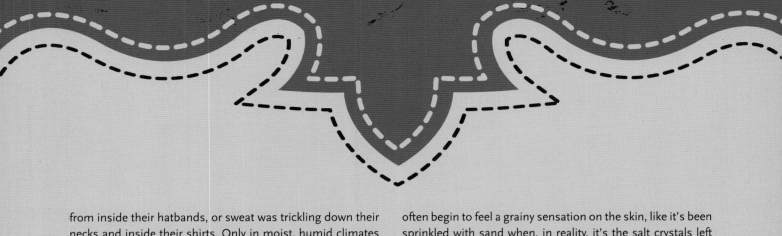

from inside their hatbands, or sweat was trickling down their necks and inside their shirts. Only in moist, humid climates would that be true. In a southern Arizona summer, the air temperature is often well over a hundred degrees and the relative humidity below ten percent. A human body can lose a great amount of water in that kind of an environment. Even though a person would be sweating a lot, the extreme dry heat would be evaporating it so fast there would be almost no sensation of perspiring. Clothing might at first become damp, but, instead of being wet with sweat, a person would often begin to feel a grainy sensation on the skin, like it's been sprinkled with sand when, in reality, it's the salt crystals left from evaporation. Dehydration would set in quickly without a person realizing it. Dizziness, headache, a spike in blood pressure and heat stroke could follow shortly thereafter.

In the above two examples of the knife blade gleaming by starlight and the frequent instances of excessive sweating, L'Amour probably knew better, yet purposely exaggerated these descriptions for dramatic effect, rather than going for factual accuracy.

Kilrone, hero of the novel by the same name, was trying to escape from a cavalry fort that was being attacked by hundreds of Bannock Indians. The attackers rode in behind a herd of horses they stampeded ahead of them. Kilrone grabbed the mane of a passing horse and leapt to its back, hanging off to one side, Indian-like, to be out of sight. He managed to escape. After he was safely away, he stopped to fashion a hackamore for the horse from some rawhide strips he carried. Ten pages later, after Kilrone has ridden the gray horse many miles and several hours without seeing anyone, the horse has mysteriously acquired a saddle.

In *North to the Rails,* Tom Chantry was helping drive a herd of cattle in a wilderness area. "The stars were out; the sky was black above, the earth was black below. The cattle were slowing now....As he had them streaming out toward the east, suddenly three riders topped out on a knoll. Instantly he recognized one of them—it was Sarah. And the Talrims!"

In the blackness, Chantry could never have even seen three riders topping a knoll some distance away, much less recognized their faces.

The Man Called Noon contained the following line: "... a pebble rolled under the sole of his boot and he fell heavily." In this scene, the man is wearing moccasins.

A thorough search would probably turn up more of these minor discrepancies. But readers and editors either missed or ignored them. The story always plunged ahead like a flash flood in a rocky canyon, carrying such small debris with it.

Top: Cattle drives rarely went more than ten or twelve miles a day, as the cattle had to be given time to rest and graze. A drive from Texas to Montana could take up to five months. **Above:** In many of his novels L'Amour described his characters as sweating profusely. However, only in moist, humid climates would that be true. In a southern Arizona summer, the air temperature is often well over a hundred degrees and the relative humidity below ten percent. **Opposite:** A classic 1888 cowboy photographed at Sturgis in the Dakota Territory. Today the historic town of Sturgis is best known as a mecca for another group of lone riders; motorcyclists.

CHAPTER 10

GOLD AND GLORY

In every human endeavor, it seems, the efforts of certain individuals are rewarded with worldly success, while the majority are stuck in mediocrity or slide into failure. What determines why a few are wildly successful and most others not? Talent? Hard Work? Fate? Help from others? A good agent? Blind chance? Divine providence? This has always been a fascinating question. In the field of writing and publishing, it is a question that has not been clearly answered, and may never be. If every aspiring writer who set pen to paper or strung sentences together on a keyboard knew the answer to this question, each one of them would be turning out bestsellers.

The question has always been even more puzzling and frustrating to publishers. The history of publishing is crammed with examples of books that were rejected over and over until finally accepted by some company and published (or even self-published in this day and time), only to become runaway bestsellers, earning the publisher and author hundreds of thousands of dollars and thrusting the author into instant fame.

Opposite: Louis L'Amour was apparently born with a talent for storytelling. He stated in his memoir that he was poor at mathematics—a common trait of many who are good at English composition. **Right:** Some other well-known western authors of the twentieth century were much more prolific than L'Amour. Max Brand (real name: Frederick Faust) wrote more than 500 novels for magazines and almost as many shorter stories. His total literary output is estimated to have been between 25,000,000 and 30,000,000 words.

Zane Grey (1872–1939) preceded L'Amour by a generation and was easily the most popular western writer of his time. *Riders of the Purple Sage* (1912) was Grey's best-selling book. In addition to the commercial success of his printed works, many of them had second lives and continuing influence when adapted as films and television productions. Interestingly, Grey was also a pioneer of American big-game saltwater fishing.

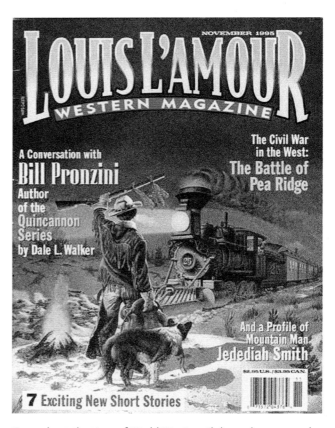

From about the time of World War I until the early 1950s, pulp magazines flourished. They were called pulps because they were printed on cheap pulp paper that turned yellow due to their acid content and deteriorated over time. Pictured is a monthly magazine named for L'Amour that existed for two years in the mid-1990s.

L'Amour was certainly not the first to achieve great status as a western author, but in the end he exceeded in fame even the wildly popular Zane Grey (1872–1939), who preceded him by a generation. These were two very different writers from two different eras, and each had millions of loyal fans, so it's probably not realistic to even compare their level of fame.

And several other well-known western authors of the twentieth century were much more prolific than either L'Amour or Grey. To name only two—Max Brand (real name: Frederick Faust) and Lauran Paine (real name: Lawrence K. Duby Jr.). Each of these men wrote hundreds of books under numerous pen names. Yet, L'Amour's lifetime output still exceeded a hundred books—a considerable number, not counting a few hundred short stories. He never had a literary agent; he dealt with publishers directly.

Three things determine the success (if not the long-term fame) of an author. They are (1) some degree of inborn talent, (2) hard work and persistence, and (3) luck (or Providence). The author has control over only the second of these.

L'Amour was apparently born with a talent for storytelling. He stated in his memoir that he was poor at mathematics—a common trait of many who are good at English composition. From the

Above: Unlike many young, aspiring writers, L'Amour was able to draw on a variety of real-life experiences and adventures for story material. In lieu of the formal education he had cut short, he spent years educating himself in the hard school of manual labor. Though he never worked as a lumberjack, L'Amour did have experience working at a lumber mill. One has to wonder how the horses in this vintage logging photo could pull that sled! **Left:** From the age of fifteen when he abandoned formal schooling, L'Amour was a voracious reader. During all the years from 1923 until after World War II when he left the roving, knockabout life and settled down in Los Angeles, Louis was reading and trying to write for publication.

time at age fifteen when he abandoned formal schooling, he was a voracious reader. During all the years from 1923 until after World War II when he left the roving, knockabout life and settled down in Los Angeles, he was reading and trying to write for publication. Success came slowly, but he finally began to sell regularly to the pulp magazines, stories of crime and adventure as well as some western tales.

From about the time of World War I until the early 1950s, pulp magazines flourished. These were the more sophisticated successors to the earlier dime novels of the late 1800s. They were called pulps because they were printed on cheap pulp paper that turned yellow due to their acid content and deteriorated over time. But, even though some people collect them today, these magazines were not intended to last. They were magazines that catered to every taste and every genre, from romance to crime to westerns to science fiction. Lurid cover art jumped out at readers passing a newsstand, begging for attention, promising adventure for as little as ten to twenty-five cents per copy. They were available nearly everywhere—newsstands, drugstores, train stations, hotel lobbies. For those who loved to read but didn't have the money for hardback books, these magazines were extremely popular. And this type of reading was not available at the local library. The stories they contained made no pretense at being great literature, but they were eye-catching and entertaining. The payment for authors of these

stories was low—as little as a penny a word, and sometimes less—and the requirements strict as to the type of story accepted. In regard to adventure stories, crime fiction, and westerns, fast action had to take precedence over character development, introspection, or detailed description.

Unlike many young, aspiring writers, L'Amour was able to draw on a variety of real-life experiences and adventures for story material. In lieu of the formal education he had cut short, he spent years educating himself in the hard school of manual labor. He was able to get hired as a deckhand on a freighter and made a trip around the world when he was about eighteen years of age, meeting all kinds of odd characters in foreign ports and aboard ship. He hitchhiked from place to place wherever he heard about a job prospect. He hopped freights, camped out in hobo jungles, worked in a lumber mill, labored in a circus, performed assessment work on isolated mining claims, planted orange trees, and worked on the docks. One of his jobs was helping skin the carcasses of cattle that had died of natural causes in order to salvage the hide for leather. It was a nauseating job and he hated it, but kept at it to earn his pay. It was a hard life he had chosen. He often found himself cold, hungry, and broke, hiking along some deserted road hoping for a ride or sleeping under the stars in a desert, one eye open for snakes, then shaking out his boots in the morning to check for scorpions.

But he retained his upbeat attitude, believing that things would change for the better. He remarked much later that, "The armchair adventurer has all the advantages, believe me. As I have said elsewhere, and more than once, I believe that adventure is nothing but a romantic name for trouble." This was a subject on which he spoke with authority. "What people speak of as adventure is something nobody in his right mind would seek out, and it becomes romantic only when one is safely at home."

Much of L'Amour's *Sitka* was set in the frozen frontier of Alaska. The story drew all brands of adventurers, con men, criminals, and pioneers—men such as trail-tough, battle-hardened Jean LaBarge. This 1898 hand-colored halftone reproduction of an illustration portrays the prospectors' dogsled in a snowstorm on their way to the Klondike goldfields.

He stated that during the booming twenties, there were more unskilled jobs than there were men to do them, so finding short-term employment was relatively easy. Big and strong for his age, he looked mature enough at age sixteen to pass for twenty-two and thus was able to fit into a world of grown working men. Some of the jobs he performed—such as longshoreman—would later require union membership.

In his autobiography L'Amour wrote of a story he heard as a sixteen-year-old while seated at a campfire in the Texas panhandle. A man in his eighties named Peterson told a remarkable story. L'Amour could not later vouch for the truth of the tale, but all the historical details seemed to check out. A brutal father had reared this man, who wasn't even sure his own name was Peterson. When the boy was twelve years old, Apaches attacked their ranch. His father fought like a tiger but was killed, and the boy expected the same fate, but one of the Apaches said that if the boy Peterson could fight like his father, he'd be spared and become an Apache. The raiders, from Nana's band, took the boy. Since he'd been used to living such a harsh life, being raised by Apaches seemed almost a relief. When he was about sixteen, several groups of Apaches, including Cochise and Victorio, banded together to plan an attack on a westbound stagecoach. More than 200 braves lay in ambush at Stein's Pass in New Mexico (near the border of present-day Arizona).

Regarding his adventurous start to life, L'Amour remarked, "The armchair adventurer has all the advantages, believe me. As I have said elsewhere, and more than once, I believe that adventure is nothing but a romantic name for trouble." Pictured is a group of travelers in the Dakota Territory around 1889.

The boy was taken along to observe and to care for the horses. The stagecoach was stopped by shooting the horses from rocky shelter on the canyon walls. Seven well-armed men were in the coach. No relief could be expected because all the US Cavalry had been withdrawn to fight in the Civil War. One of the men in the stage was killed outright, but the rest had rifles and a thousand rounds of ammunition and were able to hold off the Apaches for three days. But they had no food, little water, and were all eventually killed, but not before they had picked off over 150 of their Apache attackers.

L'Amour was amazed that he was hearing about an historic episode of the Apache wars described by an eyewitness, and stated he wished he had known at the time to ask many questions. But he had no idea he'd be using this for background in later stories.

At first reading, the old man's tale seemed rather dubious for several reasons—the Butterfield Stage Line that ran the southern route to California ceased operations when the Civil War broke out because protective troops were withdrawn to fight the war. Secondly, Apache bands seldom banded together to attack in numbers of 400–500, and why was such a huge force needed to stop one stagecoach? Apache predations did pick up when the soldiers left the southwest, but separate Apache bands usually did not combine in one attack force. Their overall objective was to terrorize whites and block their settlement on Apache lands. To accomplish this, they used hit-and-run tactics in small numbers. They were not siege fighters. It was an exciting story, but one which, even if partially true, had very probably been embellished.

However, contemporary reports written shortly after the attack verify the basic facts of this story. It happened in April 1861, in Steins Pass, New Mexico. The stagecoach party (known, for some reason, as the Free Thompson Party) were

five, six, or seven tough frontiersmen who were well armed with the latest rifles and sidearms and either 1,000 or 2,000 rounds of ammunition. There *were* several hundred Apaches under Cochise and Mangas Coloradas in the attacking party (Victorio was not mentioned). And 135 to 140 braves *were* picked off by the

Above right: L'Amour was skeptical of a fantastic tale an older gentleman told him about an Indian clash that he experienced as a teenager. After researching the story, it appears the incident may very well have happened. It involved Mangas Coloradas (pictured) and a besieged stagecoach party in 1861. **Below:** In 1881 Helen Hunt Jackson published *A Century of Dishonor*, the first detailed examination of the federal government's treatment of Native Americans in the West. Her findings shocked the nation with proof that empty promises, broken treaties, and brutality helped pave the way for white pioneers. Pictured in this lithograph is the US Cavalry pursuing Native Americans, circa 1899.

white sharpshooters. Thus, no matter how much history a person might think he knows, there will always be a true story or incident that crops up to confound him.

In his autobiography L'Amour related another such story whose veracity seemed suspect. As a young man, he had taken a short-term job doing assessment work on a mining claim in the California desert. The owner, when dropping him off at the site, warned L'Amour about a crazy old Indian who lived on another claim a mile away and might be dangerous. The Indian (whom L'Amour thought was a Papago) later showed up. He was friendly enough, but eccentric. Reportedly over ninety years old, he had only one eye. During his visit, the old man bagged his supper by taking two snap shots with his revolver. Each shot clipped the head off a different quail. L'Amour reported witnessing this marksmanship. Such marvelous off-hand pistol shooting like that by a one-eyed ninety year old, though unlikely, could have happened. The Indian might have been a natural pistol shot all his life, and some of this skill was still retained in spite of age and disability.

In his short story "The Gift of Cochise," a ten-year-old boy took a heavy Winchester rifle and, bracing it against a door frame, nailed a fruit pod on a prickly pear cactus 200 yards away. This, of course, was fiction, but L'Amour knew that such shooting was possible.

In those early days before telescopic sights, long-range shooting accuracy in the vast distances of mountains or deserts was sometimes accomplished by the use of a pop-up adjustable sight that was mounted on top of the receiver, or on the stock near the drop of the comb. A good example of this tang sight was shown being used by Tom Selleck in the movie *Quigley Down Under*. A man had to know his particular rifle to make allowances for elevation and windage.

L'Amour knew about one of the most famous long-distance shots in western history that was

Above: Pictured is Shoshoni Indian Chief Washakie, whose name has been translated in various ways. It apparently dealt with his tactics in battle as one story describes how Washakie devised a large rattle by placing stones in an inflated and dried balloon of buffalo hide, which he tied on a stick. He carried the device into battle to frighten enemy horses, earning the name "The Rattle" or "Gourd Rattler." Another translation of "Washakie" is "Shoots-on-the-Run." **Opposite:** In his autobiography L'Amour related a story whose veracity seemed a bit suspect. He told of an Indian, reportedly over 90 years old, who had only one eye. During L'Amour's visit, the old man bagged his supper by taking two snap shots with his revolver. Each shot clipped the head off a different quail.

fired by a man named Billy Dixon. The shot ended a siege by a force of over 700 Indians in June of 1874.

A small party of buffalo hunters had gathered at a place called Adobe Walls near the Canadian River in Texas. They were scouring the southern plains for a dwindling number of buffalo. But they were also encroaching on land set aside by treaty for the Indians. A combined force of Kiowa and Comanche took exception to this and decided to

August.

me out of "gas mask" like tonite.

Fri.-9- Still on job, soft job under shade tree. "Stunt" night at Batt. Hdq. much enjoyed.

Sat. 10. Easy day. Drill short. washed gas-mask & turned in. Inspection of everything Batt. parade tonite. 4th platoon shows up good.

Sun. 11- Feeling bum today. Went to ditch took bath & washed clothes. Plenty to eat today as most of Co. out on passes.

Mon.-12- Short drill this A.M. Went to range in P.M. to shoot "auto" Some fine sport. Came back & all stuff out in field. Slept in open.

August.

Tue-13- Moved from Custoza. On baggage detail & rode to Valeggio. Pitch squad tents, but had to change several times to suit Col. Whole regiment here.

Wed-14- I'm kitchen today. Bunch moved tents again today. All my stuff moved.

Notes.- Were glad to move from Custoza as we were away from everything. At Valeggio whole regi. is here & we have Red Cross & "Y"; makes life a little more interesting.

Aug.15- Hotternell, Batt. hikes thru Valeggio to river for movies. Caught hell for marching at ease

During his teens, twenties, and thirties, when Louis L'Amour was proudly making his own way, trying to find his life's work, and putting stories to paper, he kept in touch with his parents and family who had relocated to Oklahoma. He returned there to spend time with them, all the while continuing to read and attempting to write for publication. Pictured is a World War I soldier's journal.

wipe them out. They attacked the hunters who were holed up in a couple of adobe buildings. But the whites were awake and ready for the dawn attack and managed to kill a number of the attackers and drive them back. Two of the hunters and a dog were killed early in the battle that lasted two more days. With plenty of cover and long-range weapons, the few riflemen were able to withstand the hundreds of attacking hostiles, and the battle settled into a siege.

On the third morning, a group of mounted Indians gathered on a hill nearly a mile away, apparently discussing their next move. Bat Masterson, one of the hunters, suggested to Billy Dixon, former army scout and the best marksman in the company, that he attempt a shot with his "big fifty" buffalo gun—a Sharps .50 caliber. Bracing the heavy gun on a rest, Dixon carefully sighted on the distant group of Indians and fired. It took over five seconds for the bullet to reach its target, but one of the Indians suddenly toppled off his horse, either wounded or killed. The conferring chiefs decided at that point they'd had enough and called off the siege, leading their warriors away. It

Above: Around the start of the twentieth century, Wild West shows were extremely popular. Within the first two years of the first Wild West show, more than 10,000,000 spectators had seen it, and it had a profit of $100,000. Easterners were eager to enjoy the thrill and danger of the West, and in this way it was made possible to do so without the risks and consequences that came along with the real West. Of all the shows, the first, most famous, and most successful was Buffalo Bill's Wild West and Congress of Rough Riders of the World. **Right:** The United States Cavalry, or US Cavalry, was the designation of the mounted force of the United States Army from the late eighteenth to the early twentieth century. The Cavalry branch was absorbed into the Armor branch in 1950, but the term "Cavalry" remains in use in the US Army for certain armor and aviation units historically derived from cavalry units. Originally designated as United States Dragoons, the forces were patterned after cavalry units employed during the Revolutionary War. The traditions of the US Cavalry originated with the horse-mounted force, which played an important role in extending United States governance into the western United States after the American Civil War.

Above: L'Amour got very little help along his way to literary stardom. One instance where he did stuck out in his mind, and he wrote about it in his autobiography. At one time, trying desperately to write something that would sell, he rented a typewriter. Later, when he couldn't continue to pay the rent, the owner simply let him keep it. "That typewriter meant more to me than anything else that happened," he wrote. "I was able to go on working." **Right:** When the Union Pacific Railroad crossed the Great Plains, large numbers of workers, hangers-on, and purveyors of vice congregated in temporary boom communities known as "Hell on Wheels." With few towns in existence along the Union Pacific line, there was little for the men to do, so professional gamblers, saloonkeepers, and prostitutes filled the void in entertainment, building a reputation that lasts to the present. By no means, though, did all activity revolve around vice. In longer-lived towns, literary clubs, religious gatherings, theatrical offerings, and other activities were common. Two communities coexisted in the Hell on Wheels towns: the raucous railroad builders and their followers and the business-oriented class who hoped to remain and build permanent communities.

North American elk rest majestically on
a Rocky Mountain meadow in Colorado.

There are places one can still get a feel for the Old West even today. This is the front desk of an old hotel near Murdo, South Dakota.

was later determined the shot was 7/8 of a mile—1,538 yards, a remarkable feat of shooting.

In his autobiography, L'Amour mentioned while he and a friend were taking a car trip, they stopped overnight at the home of an acquaintance. In his bedroom, L'Amour discovered a copy of the book *The Life of Billy Dixon* (dictated by Dixon to his wife just before he died in 1913). Since he couldn't take the book with him the next day, L'Amour stayed up all night reading it.

L'Amour later mentioned this incident in his novel *Kilrone*. At an undermanned cavalry fort, the hero, Kilrone, and a handful of defenders were bracing for an imminent attack by Bannock Indians. A man named McCracken asked, "You reckon we got a chance?"

"We've got a good chance," Kilrone replied with an assurance he did not feel. "Look what those boys did at Adobe Walls a few years back—twenty-eight buffalo hunters stood off upwards of seven hundred Indians. Some say as many as fifteen hundred."

During his teens, twenties, and thirties when Louis L'Amour was proudly making his own way, trying to find his life's work, and putting stories to paper, he kept in touch with his parents and family who had relocated to Oklahoma. He returned there to spend time with them, all the while continuing to read and attempting to write for publication. As many aspiring writers do, he kept a notebook of pieces submitted and rejected. In later years, he seemed to be proud of being able to go it alone, struggling toward his goal of becoming a professional writer. In his autobiography, he wrote: "Times were often very rough for me, but I can honestly say I never felt abused or put-upon. I never felt, as some have, that I deserved special treatment from life, and I do not recall ever complaining that things were not better. Often I wished they were, and often found myself wishing for some sudden windfall that would enable me to stop wandering and working and settle down to simply writing. Yet it was necessary to be realistic. Nothing of the kind was likely to happen, and of course, nothing did.

"I never found any money; I never won any prizes; I was never helped by anyone, aside from an occasional encouraging word—and those I valued. No fellowships or grants came my way, because I was not eligible for any and in no position to get anything of the sort. I never expected it to be easy."

But he did record one instance of receiving help:

"There was one thing, and one man whom I have not forgotten. At one time, trying desperately to write something that would sell, I rented a typewriter. For several months I paid the rent. Then a time came when I could not, so I wrote him a note and explained. I never heard from him again. No bill, nothing. That typewriter meant more to me than anything else that happened. I was able to go on working."

When the Great Depression hit, it affected him as it did everyone else. But midway through that decade of the 1930s, he managed to sell his first story, a short-short entitled "Anything for a Pal," to *True Gang Life* magazine, and it was published in October 1935. He was paid $6.54. While living with his family in Choctaw, Oklahoma, he sold a

An 1898 view of Oklahoma Avenue in the main commercial district of Guthrie, Oklahoma. In just a few decades, early automobiles would soon be spotted on western streets such as this.

boxing story, "Gloves for a Tiger." It was sold to Standard Magazines, and appeared in the January 1938 issue of *Thrilling Adventures*. It would be a long struggle, but he'd gotten his foot in the door.

He and other itinerant laborers often memorized and recited favorite poems. A fairly large amount of well-known narrative poetry had grown up around the world of freight trains and hobos. During the Depression, thousands of men who were thrown out of work took to the rails in search of jobs that had suddenly ceased to be plentiful. Hoboing grew even larger than in the previous decade. But now the wandering way of life took on an element of desperation, replacing the carefree adventuring it had been before.

L'Amour's fascination with the power and beauty of words extended to reading and often memorizing all sorts of poetry. He was inspired to write *Smoke from This Altar,* a collection of poems, in 1939. It's possible he at least copublished this little volume.

After his army discharge, L'Amour contacted editor Leo Margulies at Standard Publications.

Mister Margulies suggested that L'Amour continue writing stories for his chain of pulp magazines. Some of the stories he wrote and submitted were published under the pen name Jim Mayo. Most of these were non-western adventures.

During this period after the war, when he struggled to write, he was living in Los Angeles and now and then spent an evening at the Brown Derby where he hung out at the bar, trading stories with friends and movie people, making himself known to actors. The rest of the time, he said, he spent between his typewriter and the Hollywood public library.

To show the circumstances of how L'Amour rose to fame above his contemporaries, we must look at the career of another western author, Luke Short. This was the pen name of Frederick D. Glidden, who was born in Illinois in 1908, the same year L'Amour was born in North Dakota. Glidden was graduated from the School of Journalism at the University of Missouri in 1930 and then faced the daunting prospect of trying to make a living during the Depression, which had just started. For the next year or so he worked at several newspapers as a reporter. Then he worked briefly in the logging industry and was a trapper in Canada before returning to the states as an archaeologist's helper in New Mexico in 1933–1934. During this time he was reading pulp westerns and decided he could write better than the stories he read there, so he began to write tales set in the Northwest where he had worked.

Through a friend, Glidden managed to contact and secure the services of a literary agent, Marguerite Harper. She advised him to set his stories in the West instead of the Northwest. The year following, 1935, she sold his first story, "Six-Gun Lawyer," to *Cowboy Stories,* a Street and Smith publication. The story was published under his name, but the editor said his name didn't sound very western. So Marguerite Harper suggested Glidden take a pen name. Luke Short was chosen.

This magnificent larger-than-life cattle drive sculpture resides at the Chisholm Trail Heritage Center in Duncan, Oklahoma. It took sculptor Paul Moore two years and countless hours of tedious, and sometimes backbreaking, work to finish the massive and eerily realistic image of the "Chisholm Trail."

It's not known for sure if either of them knew there had been a real western gunfighter by that name, a cohort of Bat Masterson, Doc Holliday, and Wyatt Earp.

Shortly after, Glidden got a break when *Adventure* magazine bought his novel *Feud at Single Shot,* and ran it as a serial in five parts during 1935.

Glidden urged his wife to write, and she did, authoring and selling western romances under a pen name, Vic Elder. She wrote until 1943 when she stopped writing to care for their three children.

Fred Glidden's brother, Jonathan, was a salesman in Illinois, and Fred urged him to come to New Mexico and write. Jonathan joined him in 1937 and began writing westerns under the pen name Peter Dawson. This name, chosen by Marguerite

Harper, was supposedly based on his favorite brand of whiskey.

From then on, Luke Short began to roll, and turned out good, saleable stories that were accepted and published, even breaking into the lucrative market of the slicks.

Because of poor eyesight, he was immune from the military draft but worked for the Office of Strategic Services. He sold western stories in England. During the 1940s, he hit his peak with nine novels serialized by *Colliers* and *The Saturday Evening Post.* His paperbacks sold in the millions. He moved to Aspen, Colorado, in 1947. Several movies were made from his books.

In 1953 he was one of the founders of Western Writers of America. But in the 1950s his career began to go downhill. He had a contract to produce two books a year for Bantam Books, but was able to produce only six books during the entire decade. Marguerite managed to persuade Bantam to allow Fred's brother, Jonathan, to write the remaining books. But Jonathan died unexpectedly in June 1957. Bantam had to use a ghostwriter to complete Fred's contract, but the book sales were less than expected.

In the late 1940s, while this had been going on, L'Amour was still hammering out stories at a furious pace for the pulps. However, in spite of his publishing record with short stories and novelette-length pieces, he had to turn to a genre publisher in England to get his first western novel accepted and into print. *Westward the Tide* was published in 1950.

After the failure of Luke Short to deliver the required number of novels, Bantam turned to L'Amour in 1955 with the same offer, asking for two books a year. He accepted. Bantam later upped this to three books a year when they realized this author was willing and capable of producing that many publishable novels. Bantam bought the rights to the two or three earlier Ace and Fawcett novels L'Amour had written and added them to his Bantam list.

As the pulps began to fade from the scene with the coming of television and the advent of paperback books (many of them novelette length), L'Amour and Bantam were off and running and never looked back. Bantam Books was to remain his publisher for the rest of his life. Even to this day, they are reprinting and selling his books.

Hitting his writing peak at this time in history, L'Amour rode the wave of popularity for the western story. During the 1950s and 1960s, the public's taste for televised westerns was greater than it has ever been, and many western serials were running weekly on TV—*Gunsmoke; Have Gun, Will Travel; Wagon Train; Johnny Yuma; The Life and Legend of Wyatt Earp; The Rifleman;*

Above: During the 1950s and 1960s, the public's taste for televised westerns was greater than it has ever been, and many western serials were running weekly on TV. One of the most popular and longest running was *Gunsmoke*, which was televised from 1955–1975 and starred James Arness as US Marshal Matt Dillon.

In spite of his publishing record with short stories and novelette-length pieces, L'Amour had to turn to a genre publisher in England to get his first western novel accepted and into print. *Westward the Tide* was published in 1950.

The Lawman; Alias Smith and Jones; Bat Masterson; Bonanza; The Big Valley; The Rebel; Sugarfoot; and *Maverick* to name just a few.

In a 2011 videotaped interview, Marc Jaffe, former editor at Bantam and longtime friend of L'Amour, related how the management at Bantam decided to boost L'Amour's star in its rising by the unusual step of not only publishing his three books a year, but also keeping all of his backlist in print and available for many new readers. The publisher had never made a commitment of this kind to any other western author but got behind L'Amour with a strong promotional campaign, spending on advertising for a genre writer who was not yet a household name.

Of course, it wasn't as if L'Amour was an unknown by the late 1950s. A charming, affable man and an able speaker, L'Amour had been active on the Los Angeles social scene since settling there in 1946, and his name often appeared in the gossip columns of newspapers. He had been dating actress Julie Newmar before meeting his future wife and marrying in 1956. Even as he continued to write crime and western stories for the pulps, his name was becoming known.

The biggest break in his writing career up to the time he signed with Bantam was the movie *Hondo* and the novelization he did from the screenplay. For greatest impact, both movie and book were released on the same day in 1953. It had begun when his short story "The Gift of Cochise" was published in the slick pages of *Colliers* magazine in 1952. Someone connected to John Wayne's new production company saw the story, which led to the company purchasing the screen rights for $4,000. A screenwriter altered the story, renamed the main character Hondo Lane (from the original Ches Lane), and the movie came out with the name *Hondo*.

L'Amour made the most of the publicity this afforded and continued his self-promotion efforts. He never missed a chance to appear on the new medium of TV, give an interview on the radio or for newspapers, or show up at a public event dressed in western hat, bolo tie, and high-heeled cowboy boots. And he always stressed his connection with the real West, relating the family story about his great-grandfather being scalped by the Sioux. Reporters sought out L'Amour for interviews because the events of his own life were as adventurous and fascinating as many of his fictional characters.

When he'd first begun to sell stories to the pulps, supposedly one of his editors suggested he might want to select a pen name since "L'Amour" didn't sound very manly. (Glamorous actress Dorothy L'Amour was a very popular pinup girl at the time in the 1940s.) Louis declined, stating that his father, Dr. L. C. LaMoore, had Anglicized the spelling from the original French, "L'Amour."

Considering all the other things he mastered in his long life, and the great effort he made to educate himself in wide areas of learning, it seemed very odd that he never learned the standard touch-typing method of writing on a typewriter. Afterall, he made his living typing. Why type with two fingers all those years? Perhaps he started that way and got so accustomed to it that he didn't want to change.

L'Amour bought a ranch in southwestern Colorado not far from the ancient cliff dwellings at Mesa Verde National Park. He spent part of the

The biggest break in L'Amour's writing career up to the time he signed with Bantam was the movie *Hondo* and the novelization he did from the screenplay. For greatest impact, both the movie and book were released on the same day in 1953.

year there, working, walking his land, and breathing in the solitude and splendor of nature. In the early 1980s he announced plans to have an actual working historic town built on his Colorado property. He intended this town not only for tourists, but also envisioned that it would be rented out as a setting for western movies, much as Old Town near Tucson has been for years. The frontier settlement, to be named "Shalako" after one of his fictitious characters, would be reminiscent of a typical western town from the late 1800s, containing a saloon, bakery, tonsorial parlor, blacksmith shop, general mercantile, church, gunsmith shop, and other businesses that would have been

Cliff dwellings are one of the more fascinating aspects of Native American life, and L'Amour spent quite a bit of time exploring the many well-preserved ruins throughout the Southwest. This is the "Long House" at Mesa Verde National Park in Colorado.

During his career, Louis L'Amour published more than 400 short stories and over one hundred novels, some of which have been translated into ten languages. In addition he wrote sixty-five TV scripts and sold over thirty stories to the motion picture industry.

found in that time and place. For various reasons, however, this grand plan never got beyond the planning stages.

In his memoir, L'Amour described the experience of spending a night with his wife and a park ranger in one of the cliff dwellings (he didn't say exactly where), and wrote about what a wonderful experience it was. Years before, in his lone wandering, he had slept in ruins and ancient cliff dwellings before laws protected those places.

During the last decade of his life, L'Amour received several prestigious awards, beginning in 1981 with the Saddleman Award from Western Writers of America. The Levi Straus Company

sponsored this award at that time, which was represented by a bronze statue of a cowboy with a saddle slung over one shoulder. The Saddleman was conferred in recognition of a lifetime achievement in furthering the lore of the West.

He also received the North Dakota Rough Rider award.

In 1982, he received a Congressional Gold Medal. And in 1984 he was awarded the Presidential Medal of Freedom. Both of these medals were presented to L'Amour in person by a fan and fellow westerner, President Ronald Reagan.

Any search of fan reviews of L'Amour's books on the internet would show quite a number of comments stating the books' appeal was not only based on the stories themselves, but on their absence of foul language and sex scenes, so common in many modern novels.

As an example, L'Amour wrote in his short story, "One for the Pot," "The old man swore savagely." But the author didn't put the swear words on the page. He left details of the old man's language to the imagination of the reader. Only now and then did "hell" or "damn" appear in dialogue on his pages. L'Amour apparently thought

Top: In the early 1980s, L'Amour made plans to have an actual working historic town built on his Colorado property. He intended this town not only for tourists, but also envisioned that it would be rented out as a setting for western movies (similar to Old Tucson Studios in Arizona). For various reasons, however, this grand plan never got beyond the planning stages. Pictured is the old Oatman (Arizona) Drug Company building which was built in 1904. It's now called the "Glory Hole," with an antique shop on the ground floor and a small museum upstairs. **Bottom:** By way of entertainment, saloons offered dancing girls, some of whom occasionally or routinely doubled as prostitutes. Many saloons offered Faro, poker, brag, three-card Monte, and dice games. Other games were added as saloons continued to prosper and face increasing competition. These additional games included billiards, darts, and bowling. Some saloons even included piano players, can-can girls, and theatrical skits.

Right: L'Amour felt it was unnecessary to be explicit when his characters swore, although one can find an occasional "hell" or "damn" in his writings. Pictured are Clint Eastwood (left) and Eli Wallach as Tuco in 1967's *The Good, the Bad, and the Ugly.* **Lower right:** In the 1987 made-for-TV movie *The Quick and the Dead,* based on the L'Amour novel by the same name, Kate Capshaw played Susanna McKaskel. Sam Elliott and Tom Conti also starred in the production.

some readers might be offended by foul language. And he was probably right. Besides compliments about the clean language from online reviewers of his stories, some readers have even inked out the words "hell" and "damn" in his paperbacks. In any case, L'Amour usually felt it was unnecessary to be explicit when his characters swore.

In regard to sexual content, even the western genre was not immune. Since the 1970s, several long series of so-called "adult" westerns written by a variety of ghostwriters under house names have been published. But these were separate and apart and made no pretense at being traditional westerns.

Those westerns that were basically "romance" stories set in the historic West were, and are, also a subcategory outside the mainstream. Interestingly, many of Zane Grey's novels were marketed as western romances and were serialized in women's magazines before they appeared in book form. But the word "romance" in regard to westerns had a slightly different connotation back then.

Some reader reviews of L'Amour's work mentioned that the violence in his books was necessary and appropriate to the story—that it was not gratuitous. L'Amour, himself, had this to say about violence:

"We hear a lot of talk these days about violence, but we forget the many generations that have grown up on stories of violence. The bloodiest of all, perhaps, were the so-called fairy tales, but I would have missed none of them and doubt if I did, yet I see little difference between Jack killing a fabled giant and Wyatt Earp shooting it out

In the 1987 film *The Quick and the Dead*, Duncan and Susanna McKaskel are a young married couple travelling to the West with their son, hoping to start a new life. Along the way, they stop in a small town where they meet a gang of bandits led by Doc Shabitt. After Duncan unintentionally angers the gang, he and Susanna flee the town, but Shabitt leads his men in pursuit of revenge. A mysterious stranger by the name of Con Vallian soon begins helping the family, protecting them from Shabitt's gang as they try to find a new home.

with an outlaw." He went on to say that violence was in our inherited tradition, and the Bible was full of it, as were the plays of Shakespeare where many characters were killed or committed suicide. "If we were to eliminate violence from our reading, we would have to eliminate all history, much of the world's great drama, as well as the daily newspaper."

He commented that some people had noted the absence of sex in his books, and stated that attitudes toward sex could change quickly from one generation to the next. He wrote:

Roughly a quarter of the cowboys who drove cattle from Texas to Kansas in the post-Civil War era were of mixed, nonwhite, ethnic backgrounds, according to the *Wichita Eagle*. Ben Hodges, a cowboy of mixed parentage, arrived in Dodge City in 1872, a drover bringing cattle from San Antonio. From there, he developed a reputation as a swindler, master forger, and cattle thief—but a highly likeable one.

"My stories are not concerned with sex but with entering, passing through, or settling wild country. I am concerned with people building a nation, learning to live together, with establishing towns, homes and bridges to the future." He went on to say that those unfamiliar with the world's literature might be surprised to learn that sex, except in its romantic sense, had little to do with 75 percent of what has been written. "My greatest complaint with present-day sexual writing," he went on, "is that nobody seems to be having any fun. Sex is an ordeal, or it is rape, or an athletic endeavor.... Many of those who choose it for subject matter linger on the most unpleasant aspects or treat it like a discovery. Actually, they needn't. It's been here all the time."

For L'Amour, graphic sex and swear words of any kind were taboo. Alcohol and violence were not. A certain amount of the latter had to be depicted in order to write adventure stories of the historic West.

He even used the town drunk, Finn McGraw, as the main character in the short story "The Defense of Sentinel." This unique tale opened up with McGraw waking from a drunken sleep in the street to discover that the town of Sentinel had been completely abandoned by the rest of its population. At first he thought the residents were playing a practical joke on him. An hour later, after a thorough search of the small settlement where he saw the completely empty livery stable and all the tracks leading east out of town toward the fort, he concluded that he actually was alone. The possibilities of being the sole occupant began to dawn on his whiskey-soaked brain. He was in charge of everything. He helped himself to the finest cigars and the best Irish whiskey from the saloon. Then he strolled into the general store, put on a new gray suit, white shirt and tie, and pulled on a nice pair of boots. Next he appropriated a new Winchester '73 rifle and loaded it. Next came a pair of fancy Colt revolvers and a belt of ammunition, followed by a double barrel shotgun and plenty of shells for it.

As he thought of his situation, his foggy memory came into focus. He recalled hearing, while he was cadging drinks the night before, a lot of talk about Apaches hitting a nearby ranch and the possibility of them raiding Sentinel. Victorio was on

When Wyatt Earp died in 1929 at age eighty, he was better known for his notorious handling of the Fitzsimmons-Sharkey boxing match than the OK Corral gunfight. An extremely flattering, largely fictionalized, bestselling biography published after his death created his reputation as a fearless lawman and cemented the legacy of the Shootout at the OK Corral, both of which last to this day.

Stage drivers pose with a beer keg shipment heading to a saloon in Cheyenne, Wyoming. Even though the most popular drink in Old West saloons was whiskey, beer was sometimes available and was often served at room temperature since refrigeration was scarce. Adolphus Busch introduced refrigeration and pasteurization of beer in 1880 with his Budweiser brand. Some saloons made their own beer.

the warpath, and the fort was east of town where all the residents had fled.

The upshot of the story was, unable to flee, he took it upon himself to fortify the town with boxes and barrels and locked doors and got all the arms and ammunition into one place where they were handy. The Apaches attacked and he held them off in a wild battle that lasted much of the afternoon and resumed the next morning. Fortifying himself with plenty of food and drinking the finest brands of whiskey, he called upon his fighting Irish heritage and defended himself and the town against the raiding Indians. He was wounded more than once and stopped the bleeding with handfuls of flour.

Finally, on the fourth day, the residents returned to Sentinel with the protection of a cavalry troop under Major Magruder. They found the town a wreck with all the good cigars and best whiskey gone. There was blood on the floor of the store and it was littered with blackened cartridge cases and empty whiskey bottles. " 'No one man could fire that many shells or drink that much whiskey,' Magruder said positively."

Then they realized that Finn McGraw had been left behind, and they went looking for his body. They found him, bloody, lying among his guns and empty bottles.

" 'Dead!' Carter said, 'But what a battle!'

Magruder bent over the old man, then he looked up, a faint twinkle breaking the gravity of his face. 'Dead, all right,' he said. 'Dead *drunk*!' "

Besides having his characters drinking alcohol, L'Amour even depicted a character, Tom

Previous page: The very term saloon conjures up a picture within our minds of an Old West icon, complete with a wooden false front, a wide boardwalk flanking the dusty street, a couple of hitchin' posts, and the always-present swinging doors brushing against the cowboy as he made his way to the long polished bar in search of a whiskey to wet his parched throat. Right: One of the more spectacular natural landmarks of the West is Horseshoe Bend, which is located within the Glen Canyon National Recreation Area. It's an unusual meander of the Colorado River and is located five miles downstream from the Glen Canyon Dam and Lake Powell.

Gatty, in the novel *Hanging Woman Creek,* as being addicted to patent medicines (which were normally made with a generous portion of alcohol, while some also contained opium and cocaine). Gatty, holed up in a line shack, found and read a copy of a catalog, *Home Medical Advisor.* He became convinced he had all the ailments described in this publication and thereafter began to take every patent medicine he could lay his hands on, including Dr. Robertson's Stomach Elixir, Peter's Pills, Dr. Fahnestock's Celebrated Vermifuge and Vegetable Balsam. This last was his favorite.

In spite of everything, it seems doubtful that L'Amour's degree of fame could be fully explained by years spent pounding out millions of words in his two-fingered typing style, his tireless self-promotion, Bantam's support and publicity, the movies made from his novels, and the temper of the times in which he wrote. Fame is more than the sum of its parts. There will always be an unexplainable quality about it. His incredible fame rose and roared away like a crowning forest fire, exploding from treetop to treetop, creating its own draft, engulfing everything in its path. Its momentum was unstoppable. For a man who at one time could not pay the rent on his typewriter, it was a grand finish.

Whether a reader believed that L'Amour's writing was worse than, as good as, or better than any other author of western fiction is, of course, strictly a subjective judgment. Literary critics have found fault with such things as unimaginative sameness of plots, grammatical and syntactical errors, frequent violations of the narrative point of view, and discrepancies in keeping track of details in his stories.

But nothing succeeds like success. He stated that he wrote for his readers, not for critics. He had no use for critics who considered frontier stories, or westerns, as lowbrow writing, not even worthy of reviews. L'Amour rose above the pack, and his many loyal fans continue to buy and read his works almost a generation after his death. Louis seemed especially pleased by the response from readers who actually experienced the Old West, writing, "And I am amply repaid when any old-timer, and there have been many, can put his finger on a line and say, 'Yes, that is the way it was.'"

Since L'Amour passed away from cancer in June 1988, readers of westerns might wonder why some publishing company has not tried to create another phenomenon like him. Apparently, it has been tried a time or two but was not successful. The combination of circumstances simply could not be duplicated.

Above top: Native American themes were useful in the marketing of patent medicines since Indians were thought to be in tune with nature and heirs to a body of traditional lore about herbal remedies and natural cures. Patent medicines of the late 1800s also gave rise to the term "snake oil salesman" since some of these dubious elixirs claimed to contain actual snake oil.

Above bottom: L'Amour depicted a character in *Hanging Woman Creek* as being addicted to patent medicines. In the Old West, patent medicines were typically made with a generous portion of alcohol, while some also contained opium and cocaine.

If L'Amour had any affiliation with organized religion, he kept it to himself, but his heroes exhibited moral rectitude and virtues that could be admired. Whatever names and physical descriptions he gave them in his various stories, his heroes were honest, skillful, upright, brave, strong, and considerate of women and children. Like John Wayne, who played some of these men on screen, L'Amour's protagonists exhibited what many came to consider the best American values.

In his memoir, *Education of a Wandering Man*, the last book he worked on, Louis wrote, "I have told many [stories], yet when I go down that last trail, I know there will be a thousand stories hammering at my skull, demanding to be told."

Very likely true. But for those he *did* tell, we are forever in his debt.

THE END

INDEX

Agua Caliente Indian Reservation, 98–99
alcohol, 168–169
animals, 19, 23
"Anything for a Pal" (L'Amour), 158–159
Apache wars, 147–149, 151
Arbuckle, John and Charles, 124
Arches National Park, 105
Arness, James, 161

barbed wire, 76, 79
Bell Rock, 99
Bellah, James Warner, 15
Bendigo Shafter (L'Amour), 134
Blizzard of 1886–1887, 76–77, 78, 79
Booth, John Wilkes, 53
"Booty for a Badman" (L'Amour), 113
Brand, Max (Frederick Faust), 141, 142
Broadwell, Dick, 57
Bryce Canyon National Park, 129
Bullion, Laura, 86
Busch, Adolphus, 169

Calamity Jane, 84
Capshaw, Kate, 166
Cassidy, Butch, 86
cattle, 72, 73–74, 76, 78, 79
"Celebrated Jumping Frog of Calaveras
    County, The" (Twain), 117
Century of Dishonor, A (Jackson), 149
Chilkoot Pass, 66
Chisholm Trail, 78, 160
chuckwagons, 112, 113
Civil War, 44–45, 47, 49
Clanton Gang, 138
clothes, 121, 122
Cody, William F. "Buffalo Bill," 61, 127
coffee, 111, 113, 124–125
Cold Mountain, 54
Colt, Samuel, 50–53
Colt 1873 revolver (Peacemaker), 48–49, 52, 56
Comstock Lode, The (L'Amour), 69, 119, 121
Conagher (L'Amour), 22, 24–25
Concord coaches, 116, 117–119
Conestoga wagons, 115, 116
Congressional Gold Medal, 164
Connelly, Charles, 57
Crofutt, George, 28
Crook, George, 88
Crossfire Trail (L'Amour), 123
Custer, George, 92–93

Dalton Gang, 57, 58
Dawson, Peter, 160
Daybreakers, The (L'Amour), 93, 113, 121
Death Valley Days, 121
"Defense of Sentinel, The" (L'Amour), 168–169
Delicate Arch, 105
Derringer, 53
"Desert Death Song" (L'Amour), 107
deserts, 28
Devils Tower, 14–15
Dixon, Billy, 151–152
Dodge City Police Commissioners, 55
Doolin, Bill, 61
Dougherty wagons, 116

doughnuts, 111, 131
"Dutchman's Flat" (L'Amour), 134

Earp, Morgan, 55
Earp, Virgil, 55, 61, 138
Earp, Wyatt, 55, 61, 81, 138, 168
Eastwood, Clint, 33, 34, 48–49, 56, 166
Education of a Wandering Man (L'Amour),
    101, 173
Elam, Jack, 128
Elder, Vic, 160
Elliott, Sam, 128, 166
Esitoya ("Grey Leggings"), 89

Feud at Single Shot (Short), 160
firearms, 43–44, 47, 50–54, 56
Ford, Charley and Robert, 58
Ford, Glenn, 128
Ford, John "Rip," 60–61

Geronimo, 88, 90–91
Giants in the Earth (Rolvaag), 21
"Gift of Cochise, The" (L'Amour), 130–131,
    132, 151, 163
Glen Canyon National Recreation Area, 172
Glidden, Frederick D. (Luke Short), 159–161
Glidden, Jonathan, 160–161
Glidden, Joseph, 79
"Gloves for a Tiger" (L'Amour), 159
Good, the Bad, and the Ugly, The, 166
Goodnight, Charles, 76, 78–79, 112
Graham-Tewksbury feud, 74
Grand Canyon National Park, 114
Great Depression, 158–159
Great Plains, 19, 21–22, 24–25
Grey, Zane, 15, 142, 166
Grierson, Colonel, 89
Gunsmoke, 161

Hanging Woman Creek (L'Amour), 21–22, 35,
    59, 76, 81–82, 111, 172, 173
Haroney, Mary Katherine "Big Nose Kate,"
    80–81
Haroney, Wilhelmina, 80–81
Harper, Marguerite, 159–161
Hell on Wheels towns, 154–155
Helmcken Falls, 24
Hemingway, Ernest, 134
Henry repeating rifles, 49
Hickok, Wild Bill, 52, 101, 133
Hodges, Ben, 167
Holliday, Doc, 61, 62, 81, 138
homes, 20, 21
Homestead Act (1862), 78
Hondo, 130–131, 132, 162–163
horses, 93, 95, 97, 113–114, 116, 129
Horseshoe Bend, 172
Hunting Trips of a Ranchman (Roosevelt), 78
Hyman, Mannie, 62

Iron Marshal, The (L'Amour), 35, 93, 133, 134

Jackson, Helen Hunt, 149
Jaffe, Marc, 162
James, Frank, 46–47
James, Jesse, 46–47, 58, 59
Jeremiah Johnson, 51
Johnson, Ben, 128
Jungle, The (Sinclair), 72

Kearny, Phil, 63
Ketchum, Black Jack, 132
Key-Lock Man, The (L'Amour), 134, 137
Kilkenny (L'Amour), 34
Kilrone (L'Amour), 34, 36, 44, 51, 89, 90, 128–
    129, 138–139, 158

Lando (L'Amour), 18–19, 53, 69
Langtry, Lillie, 82
language, 127–129, 131, 164, 166
Last Stand at Papago Wells (L'Amour), 26,
    28–29, 34, 134, 137
Lee, Robert E., 63
LeMat, 54
Leone, Sergio, 33, 34
Life of Billy Dixon, The (Dixon), 158
Lincoln, Abraham, 53
Little Bear, 94
Lonely Men, The (L'Amour), 82, 93, 107, 137
Loving, Oliver, 76
Lynn, Wiley, 62

Maddox, George, 36–37
Madsen, Chris (Rormose), 59, 61
Man Called Noon, The (L'Amour), 30–31, 139
Man from the Broken Hills, The (L'Amour), 134
Man from Skibbereen, The (L'Amour), 21, 35, 41
Margulies, Leo, 159
Masterson, Bat, 55, 61
Matagorda (L'Amour), 18, 19, 123
McCall, Jack, 133
McCarroll, Bonnie, 84
McKinn, Santiago, 88
Merwin-Hulbert, 53
Mesa Verde National Park, 100, 163, 164
mesas, 29–31
miners, 66
Minnie ball, 50
Mojave Crossing (L'Amour), 31, 108–109
Mojave Desert, 28
Moore, Paul, 160
Mountain Meadows Massacre, 42–43
mud wagons, 119

Nelson, John Young, 126–127
Newmar, Julie, 162
North Dakota Rough Rider award, 164
North to the Rails (L'Amour), 39, 43–44, 57, 73,
    87, 89, 134, 139

Oakley, Annie, 85
OK Corral Shootout, 56, 63, 81, 138, 168
Old Fort Defiance, 96
Old Man and the Sea, The (Hemingway), 134
"One for the Pot" (L'Amour), 164
ore wagons, 119, 121–122
Oregon Trail, 118
Osterhage, Jeff, 128
Overton, Eugene, 133

Paine, Lauren (Lawrence K. Duby Jr.), 142
Palm Canyon, 27
Parker, Isaac, 61
Parker, Quanah, 90–91
patent medicines, 172, 173
Petrified Forest National Park, 128
Pickens, Slim, 128
Place, Etta, 86
plants, 104–105, 107

Pleasant Valley War, 74
Plummer, Henry, 57
Pony Express, 146
Powers, Bill, 57
Presidential Medal of Freedom, 164
prospectors/miners, 39–41, 64–65, 68, 69–71, 113–114
pulp magazines, 142, 146, 159

Quick and the Dead, The (L'Amour), 21, 25, 136–137, 166, 167
Quigley Down Under, 151

Ranch Life and the Hunting Trail (Roosevelt), 78
ranching, 67, 69, 73–74, 78, 79
Reagan, Ronald, 164
Remington, 51, 52
Remington, Frederic, 123
Ride the River (L'Amour), 123
Riders of the Purple Sage (Grey), 142
"Riding On" (L'Amour), 30
riverboats, 123
Rivers West (L'Amour), 123
Rockies, 23, 25–26
Rolvaag, O. E., 21
Roosevelt, Theodore, 61, 78, 79, 90
Roughing It (Twain), 117

Sacketts, The, 128
Saddleman Award, 164
saloons, 165, 170–172

sandstorms, 27, 28–29
Selleck, Tom, 128, 151
Sharps, 54
sharpshooting, 151–152, 158
sheepherders, 74, 75, 78–79
Shirreffs, Gordon D., 28
Short, Luke, 61, 159–161
Sinclair, Upton, 72
Sitka (L'Amour), 147
"Six-Gun Lawyer" (Short), 159
Smith, Archie, 68
Smith & Wesson, 51, 52, 54
Smoke from This Altar (L'Amour), 159
soldiers, 44–45, 47
Spencer carbine, 48–49
Spencer repeating rifle M 1860, 48–49, 56
Springfield carbine, 54
stagecoaches, 116, 117–119
Steins Pass, 149
Stuart, Granville, 76
Sundance Kid, 86

Taggart (L'Amour), 26, 84, 86, 132, 134
Thomas, Henry Anderson "Heck," 59, 62–63
Three Guardsmen, The, 59
Tilghman, Bill, 59, 61–62
Tinajas Altas, 29
Trail Dust Town, 113
trains, 120, 154
"Trap of Gold" (L'Amour), 132
Twain, Mark, 117
typewriter, 154, 158

Under the Sweetwater Rim (L'Amour), 19, 25–26, 35–36, 87, 89, 108
Unforgiven, 48–49, 56
Union Pacific Railroad, 154
Union Stockyards, 72
US Cavalry, 153

Valley of Fire, 16–17
vigilantes, 41–42
Virginian, The (Wister), 33

Walker Colt, 51
Wallach, Eli, 166
"War Party" (L'Amour), 134
Washakie, Chief, 151
water sources ("tanks"), 27, 29
Wave, The, 16
Wayne, John, 36, 130–131, 132, 163, 173
western migrations, 20, 21, 28
Westward the Tide (L'Amour), 161, 162
whiskey, 137
White, Rollin, 50–51
Wild Bunch, 86
Wild West shows, 153
Wilderness Hunter, The (Roosevelt), 78
wildlife, 100, 101, 105, 106
Winchester Model 1886, 48–49
Winchester rifles, 56
Wister, Owen, 33

Young, Brigham, 127

PHOTO CREDITS

About the Author

Tim Champlin was born John Michael Champlin in Fargo, North Dakota, not far from where Louis L'Amour was born Louis Dearborn LaMoore twenty-nine years earlier. Louis left high school at age fifteen in the middle of his sophomore year when his father moved the family to Oklahoma. Tim also left high school at age fifteen in the middle of his sophomore year when his father was transferred from Missouri to Arizona.

But, unlike Louis, Tim did not strike out on his own. He returned to school in Phoenix and graduated from St. Mary's in 1955 before moving to Tennessee. After earning a Bachelor's degree in English from Middle Tennessee State College, he declined an offer to become a Border Patrol Agent with the US Immigration service in order to finish work on his Master of Arts degree in English at Peabody College (now part of Vanderbilt University).

After thirty-nine rejection slips, he finally sold his first piece of writing in 1971 to *Boating* magazine. The photo article, "Sailing the Mississippi," is a dramatic account of a three-day, seventy-five-mile solo adventure on the big river from Memphis to Helena, Arkansas, in a sixteen-foot fiberglass sailboat built from a kit in his basement. His only means of propulsion were the current, sails, and a canoe paddle.

Since then, thirty-six of his historical novels have been published. Most are set in the frontier West. A handful touch on the Civil War. Other books deal with juvenile time travel, a clash between Jack the Ripper and Annie Oakley, the lost Templar treasure, and Mark Twain's hidden recordings.

Besides books, he's written several dozen short stories and nonfiction articles, plus two children's books.

Tim has twice been runner-up for a Spur Award from Western Writers of America, once for a novel (*The Secret of Lodestar*) and once for a short story ("Color at Forty-Mile").

Tim is still creating enthralling new tales, and many of his books are available online as ebooks.

In 1994, he retired after thirty years of work in the US Civil Service. He is married to the former Mary Ellen Hosey, and they have three grown children and ten grandchildren. Active in sports all his life, his hobbies still include biking, shooting, sailing, and tennis.